DEPARTMENT OF HEALTH AND SOCIAL SECURITY

Social Workers and Solicitors in Child Care Cases

by Linden Hilgendorf
Tavistock Institute of Human Relations

with the assistance of
Deborah Holland
Barrie Irving
Diana Schlaefli

LONDON   HER MAJESTY'S STATIONERY OFFICE

Any views expressed in this report are those of the author
and not of the Department of Health and Social Security.

HER MAJESTY'S STATIONERY OFFICE

Government Bookshops

49 High Holborn, London WC1V 6HB
13a Castle Street, Edinburgh EH2 3AR
41 The Hayes, Cardiff CF1 1JW
Brazennose Street, Manchester M60 8AS
Southey House, Wine Street, Bristol BS1 2BQ
258 Broad Street, Birmingham B1 2HE
80 Chichester Street, Belfast BT1 4JY

*Government publications are also available
through booksellers*

ISBN 0 11 320579 X

Summary

This report describes the findings of a study of child care cases where an application is made to the courts to vary parental rights. The main focus of the study was on care proceedings under S.1.2 Children and Young Persons Act 1969. Other proceedings were also included, namely criminal prosecutions where a care order was recommended (S.7.7 Children and Young Persons Act 1969); wardship cases; applications following parental opposition to resolutions made under S.2 1948 Children Act; and applications to vary or discharge a care order. The study took place in five local authorities. Interviews were conducted with a sample of 150 social workers and a sample of 50 private solicitors. Data on 72 cases were collected from various sources including records, interviews and observation of court hearings. The variations in local conditions and arrangements which occur from one authority to another were considered insofar as they affected the handling of childcare cases. The study was conducted under a two year research grant from the Department of Health and Social Security between 1978 and 1980.

When it is decided to make an application to a court in a childcare case a decision-making process is begun in which the court hearing is only the final stage. Many individuals from various organisations are involved in the process, with a local authority social worker usually playing a major part throughout. The role demands made on social workers are complex and sometimes conflicting. Although many express anxiety and uncertainty about these cases, social workers are relatively unaware of the true complexity of their own roles. Some training and help is available but the development of support systems is patchy and generally inadequate.

The solicitor who handles childcare cases in the legal department of the local authority plays an important part in the decision-making process. Although this function has become increasingly important, sufficient attention has not been given to the nature of the role or the relationship with the social services department. The organisational structure, the role definition and the task allocation between social workers and the solicitor varies from one authority to another and is often poorly understood by social workers. Tension in the relationship between the local authority solicitor and social workers can develop and if not dealt with, can affect the preparation of cases and the presentation of evidence in court. Developing the relationship can be difficult because of the short time solicitors stay in post, although when the matter is tackled jointly good relations can be achieved.

Private solicitors are involved in many childcare cases which go to court. The role of the solicitor in care proceedings, where solicitors represent the child rather than the parents, is unclear. By preparing the case and using advocacy skills to test evidence, the solicitor can play an important part,

assisting the court by bringing out relevant information. There is less agreement about whether a solicitor should make a decision to oppose a case or to support the local authority's recommendation in the absence of instructions from his client. In practice many solicitors do take a stance one way or the other. Although individual solicitors reach their own solution to the role problems involved, there is no general consensus about their proper role or relationship with the social services department. In many cases solicitors come to represent the child as a result of social workers arranging representation. In other cases, the parents may approach the solicitor or the court may operate a rota or duty scheme. Solicitors are dependent on the social services department for information about a case. Except where a solicitor has good personal relationships with the local area office, social workers are cautious about giving information to solicitors. They are often uncertain about what information should be given and suspicious about how it will be used.

The decision to make an application to a court involves inter-agency liaison. Information is gathered and shared and a case conference is often held, particularly in non-accidental injury cases. The decision is often taken under real or perceived crisis conditions with the child being removed from home on a place of safety order. It is normally two to three months before a case is fully heard in court, although some cases may not be settled for much longer. Administrative and organisational reasons often contribute to the delay. Very long delays can occur if there are concurrent criminal prosecutions of the parents.

The physical and organisational setting of juvenile courts vary widely and some are far from satisfactory. Waiting areas, in particular, can be uncomfortable and crowded, with people waiting for both criminal and care cases. Large, old-fashioned magistrates courts are still used for care proceedings in some places. Good modern facilities, where care cases are separately scheduled, can significantly improve the experience of going to court of all the participants. The length of time taken to hear a case varies widely depending on how many witnesses are called. Many are quite short, a third of the cases observed took less than one hour. Procedural anomalies of various kinds occur in the hearings, of which the most common was the failure to distinguish between proving the facts and deciding on the disposition of the case. The social enquiry report plays an extremely important role in care proceedings but there is a need for the structure and style of reporting to be developed and the use of the report to be clarified. It is most unusual for the juvenile court not to accept that the case has been proved and to agree with the local authority recommendation. There is sometimes reason to suppose that the court is in practice only 'rubber stamping' local authority decisions. However the court does act as a control on local authority decision-making since some cases are not proceeded with because the evidence is thought to be insufficient.

Other types of proceedings in the juvenile court, particularly opposition to section 2 resolutions and applications to discharge a care order, are comparatively rare. There is considerable uncertainty as to procedures to use in these cases. Wardship procedures are sometimes used, either because other high court orders have been made in respect of the child or there are thought to be special circumstances which make other proceedings inappropriate. Ward-

ship cases may take many months to settle and the outcome is often the result of a negotiated agreement. The specificity of the orders which can be made by the court seems to be the principal advantage of the wardship procedure.

In concluding the report, the system is looked at diagnostically and a range of specific suggestions are made. These include:- comparatively minor improvements to the physical settings of juvenile courts; separate scheduling of care cases; the need for the procedure as laid down in the CYPA 1969 to be adhered to; parents to be encouraged and helped to take part in proceedings; the legal profession to consider the proper role of the representative of the child; clarification of the role of case conferences and consideration of possible alternatives; training for social workers in their roles; further development of support systems for social workers relating to the court; procedures and policies to govern the relationships with the local authority solicitor and private solicitors; a development exercise on the social enquiry report; and the juvenile court to have a wider range of disposal options.

In principle, the aim should be to shift the operational bias of the system to encourage planning for the future placement and care of the child in view of the alternatives which are realistically available; to allow decisions to be made which minimize disruption and delay in the placement of the child; and to ensure that the rights of the parents are respected and their access to a fair and full hearing by an independent court is guaranteed.

Contents

Chapter I   Introduction

When children come into the care of the local authority social workers from social service departments are usually involved in all stages of the decision-making processes. Where an application for a care order is made by the social services department a social worker will be involved in the decision to take proceedings, the preparation of the case, writing reports for court and the court hearing itself. In cases where the initiative is taken by another agency (for example, by the police) or by an individual (for example in wardship cases) the social worker may have a more restricted but still important role. Similarly when an application is made to revoke an existing care order (with the exception of those which are mainly a formality) a decision-making process is initiated in which the social worker is likely to be involved.

Decisions on care orders (whether to make, vary, not to make, or to revoke a care order) are ultimately made by a court. But this is only the final point of a process of decision-making. Although it is not always easy to identify a precise point in time at which the process begins there is always an initiating phase in which the need to take a case to court is considered. This may take the form of a rapid response to an emergency situation. Alternatively there may be a prolonged period of discussion, evaluation and contingency assessment. Once the decision to take action has been made there is a further phase of case preparation which may include obtaining interim court orders. These early phases determine the shape of the case which is finally put before the court and the nature of the decision which the court is asked to make. They are in practice an integral part of the decision-making in the case.

Although decision-making about the care of a child continues after a care order has been made, for example in relation to assessment and placement, for the purposes of this study the court hearing has been defined as the end of the process. In some instances cases do not reach the court at all. In such cases the decision not to proceed any further had been regarded as one possible outcome of the decision-making process.

The decision to apply for or to recommend a care order is one which social workers often find difficult to make and a source of considerable anxiety. The need to make such a decision does not occur very often in the overall work pattern of social work offices even though a significant number of care orders are made nationally each year. The decision may have to be taken under emergency conditions or under pressure from other agencies such as the police. Social services departments are also subject to public scrutiny of their actions in this area. On the one hand public opprobrium and formal enquiries may follow if a child is seriously injured or killed when the social services fail to protect the child by removing it from its parents. On the other they may be held equally to be at fault if they are seen to intervene unnecessarily. They

must be available to act in emergency situations or when all other actions have failed, yet always with the knowledge that there is criticism of the quality and cost of the care which they can offer a child. In addition to the inherent difficulties and anxieties in the decision to remove a child from its parents, cases of this type involve social workers in transactions with the courts and the legal profession with which they are relatively unfamiliar and often unsympathetic.

The decision-making system involving children being taken into care is complex. Depending on the type of case, there are a number of agencies, organisations and professional groups which may be involved; social service departments, education authorities, courts, various parts of the National Health Service, police, solicitors' practices, etc. The different organisations and professions have varying responsibilities, powers and professional practices. The national system of laws and administrative directions issued by government departments constrains and determines the interactions and relationships between the groups. However there is also considerable scope for local variation and the exercise of individual discretion. Individuals and groups develop their own ways of doing things, exercise their discretion in individual ways and find particular solutions to problems they encounter. This may occur in a planned and conscious way when joint committees are used to develop specific procedures, but it also occurs informally.

Even the most cursory comparison of different areas of the country reveals considerable differences between the way local systems function[1]. However it is also characteristic of locally evolving systems for managing inter-agency decision-making that those belonging to the system are unaware of its idiosyncrasies. Unless they move from one area to another people tend not to realise that there are other ways of handling matters. Much of current comment on the system suffers from a failure to recognise the extent of local variations. In particular, knowledge of the system in London is an inadequate basis for generalisations to the rest of the country. The design of this study placed special emphasis on the need to understand the local system as the context in which decisions to take children into care were made. A number of different local environments were studied so that some of the ways the system can develop could be described and in order to differentiate between features of the decision-making system which were local and those which were more general in character.

The study was designed to focus on inter-agency and inter-professional role relations, in particular between social workers and solicitors. Major inquiries following the death of a child (e.g. Maria Colwell (1974), Karen Spencer (1978) and Wayne Brewer (1977)) have frequently identified failures in communication as having been a feature of the case. Of course, in analysing a particular case *post hoc* it cannot be concluded that such failures were either causal or even a unique feature of the way the case developed. Inter-agency and inter-professional communication must be an area of concern in complex social structures and research projects have focussed on the links between social

---

[1] For example, Priestley et al (1977) describes the variations in two local systems for police decisions in respect to juveniles.

2

workers and other professional groups. (See for example, Hallett and Stephenson (1980)).

The relationships between solicitors and social workers are of particular concern in child care cases for a number of reasons:

(a) Removing children from the care of their parents is an area of social work decision-making which is subject to legal scrutiny and the decision is made by the courts. The local authority is required to prove a case in relation to defined criteria. The parties are able to test and refute evidence and the decision is subject to appeal. In using the courts in this way both the legal profession and social workers have specific roles to play in decisions affecting the welfare of children.

(b) The development of legislation which attempts to promote the welfare of citizens (to act in their best interests) has put legal institutions and lawyers under pressure to modify traditional approaches to ethical and professional problems. For example, the solicitor's role stance 'I take instructions from my client' is no longer tenable when representing a baby or a mentally ill person. The demands on the lawyer have changed gradually and have received little explicit attention. One view is that a lawyer has no place in areas of law to do with the family and in particular in divorce, since the 'legal' attitudes he brings to the role exacerbates and even creates problems. The nature of his role in areas of welfare law needs to be studied if the lawyer is to play a significant and appropriate part in cases of this type.

(c) The Children and Young Persons Act (1969) was enacted after consider-able public debate and to some extent represents a compromise between the wish to remove all decisions relating to children from the ambit of the courts and the desire to retain a legal model. The Act sits uneasily between the need to act in the best interests of the child and the need to provide a legal procedure when the rights of citizens are affected. For example the legal model is preserved in requiring the applicant to prove specific grounds (proper development, moral danger, etc.) but the welfare model is introduced with the more general test that the child is in need of care and control. The inherent ambiguity is particularly apparent in relation to the decision to make the child a party to the proceedings, but not the parents. The unresolved tension between legal and welfare considerations is bound to affect those who operate the system and particularly the way lawyers and social workers perceive and relate to each other.

In summary, this study is concerned with the decision to take a child into the care of a local authority under a court order. The decision is not seen as a unitary event but as a process which may take place over a long period and involve many individuals, professional groups and agencies. The decision making process largely takes place in local areas and in each area a decision making system for handling the process can be identified and described. Despite the existence of national laws and administrative controls there is considerable variation in the way these local systems have developed. Social workers and solicitors play crucial roles in the decision making system and this study has focussed on their roles and role relationships both generally and through their variation across local decision making systems.

The orientation of this report is that of applied social science. The study

3

aimed to describe the functioning of a social system and to identify problems which are being encountered in the operation of that system.

In the past decade there have been instances when the sytem has failed to protect individual children at risk, and these instances have provoked extreme public concern. The failures identified by inquiries into those cases need to be seen in the context of how the normal range of cases are handled. While there seems to be no reason to suppose that the 'wrong' decisions are taken in more than a very small number of cases, any system which fails unexpectedly should be investigated systematically to see whether it suffers from some inherent weaknesses. In a very complex system of multiple interacting parts it is unlikely that we can say that any given weakness will cause a particular failure because various feedback and compensating systems may act to prevent failure in particular cases. However if ways are found to improve the system by reducing friction, building in checks, increasing the understanding of those who operate it then there are likely to be fewer ways in which it will fail.

The system is under pressure to change. (See for example, Morris et al (1980); Taylor et al (1979)). If changes are to be considered they should be looked at in the light of the way the system is in fact functioning and not according to how it is supposed to function or how it functions in one area alone.

Methodology

The design of the study was based on the assumption that the decision-making process in relation to a child being taken into the care of the local authority would be a function of:

(a) the facts and circumstances of the family and child; i.e. the nature of the problems of the family, their severity or persistence and the risks involved;

(b) the national and local system for handling cases, the local rules, procedures, practices and agency organisation;

(c) the communication networks, expectations, perceptions and role definitions of the professionals involved.

In order to identify the systematic properties in cases, each of which appears totally individual, information was needed about all of these determinants. The data collection methods had to be appropriate for each type of information.

The design therefore included the following components:

(a) *Local system studies:* five local authority areas were selected and studied as operating systems. Anthropological/social geography methods were used to collect information from records, from interviews with knowledgeable informants, and by observation of interactions between participants.

(b) *Sample surveys:* within each area a sample of relevant cases were identified and followed during the decision-making process. In each case information was compiled on the character of the case using files, records and when necess-

4

ary, interviews. Data was also collected on the progress of each case using records and interviews and, when possible, observation of court hearings.

A number of methodological problems were encountered.

(a) For practical reasons the study was conducted in the areas sequentially, although there was some overlap. Because of the exploratory nature of the study the data with which we were concerned could not be entirely defined at the outset and during the course of field studies matters emerged as worthy of attention which had not been recorded in the earlier work. Rather than discard the new data it seemed desirable to include it even if there was not comparable information in all cases or areas. Thus while the majority of data is comparable across all areas and cases, in some instances more detail is available than in others.

(b) During the course of the study some significant changes were made in the law. Particularly noteworthy was the change in the legal aid rules concerning the payment of barristers. Various judgements made in relation to the use of wardship and resolutions made under S.2 of the Children Act, 1948 also began to affect decisions made by local authorities.[1] These changes could potentially have affected the findings in cases studied after they were introduced.

(c) The relationship between solicitors and social workers has not been the subject of explicit consideration by either group. Individuals from both groups tend not to have reached clearly articulated opinions about the nature of the relationship. However both groups are highly verbally skilled and sensitive to any suggestions or clues offered by the interviewer. This created methodological problems for the design of questionnaires. It was imperative that questions were formulated within the frame of reference of the respondent and without giving him guidance as to what he should reply, otherwise the responses obtained would lack both reliability and validity. With these considerations in mind, and after pilot interviewing, it was decided to use mainly open-ended questions.

(d) The study was conducted in five local authority areas and each was found to have different characteristics. It seems likely that if more areas had been included we would have found yet more variation. Perhaps every single area is unique. Nevertheless the data available on the variations and similarities between the authorities studied allows the identification of important characteristics of the system as well as some of the ways in which the system can vary.

Field Studies

The five local authorities were selected with reference to a number of criteria: authority type (London borough, metropolitan district and non-metropolitan county); geographical location; the extent to which they were affected by local authority reorganisation in 1974; and by reference to census information on population age structure, proportion of vulnerable groups, employment and housing. The aim of selection was to achieve a set of authorities of contrasting

---

[1] See in particular—Re D. (1978) *The Times*, 14 Feb. 1978; Re H (1978) 2. *W.L.R.* 608; and Johns v. Jones (1978) reported in *Family Law* 8.5.139 and 8.6.161.

types. Within general groupings, authorities were approached to take part in the study. The five authorities are described in the next chapter.

For the study to take place it was essential to obtain the co-operation of the social services department in the authority and the initial approach was made to the director. Meetings were usually held with senior members of the department and the details of the project discussed. These meetings also provided an opportunity to obtain the views of senior personnel on issues raised by the study. Contact was subsequently made with area directors (or officers) and similar discussions took place. Area directors consulted their staff about participating in the project following their normal practices, on occasions inviting members of the research team to attend a meeting with staff.

In the two urban authorities all the area teams were included in the study. However in the three large rural authorities it was decided that to reduce travelling time and cost a further selection of areas within each authority should be made. Social services departments advised the research team about which areas would be most willing to participate and the set which would best represent the variety of operating conditions in the county.

In order to collect information on the local system a number of activities were carried out:

(1) Central and area based social services personnel were interviewed including, when relevant, courts officers, team leaders, specialist child care officers, research officers, and those with responsibility for resources;

(2) In the local authority legal department solicitors handling child care cases were interviewed. Sometimes discussions were held with senior members of the department. In addition further opportunities for discussions with the solicitors also occurred in and around court hearings;

(3) Information was collected on practices, procedures and operating systems, e.g. handbooks for non-accidental injury cases;

(4) Demographic statistics, council minutes and other local information sources were investigated for any material relevant to the project;

(5) Observations were made of the location, layout, physical character and operating procedure of all the juvenile courts in which cases in the sample were heard. This involved 19 juvenile courts in all;

(6) Opportunities were taken, where an invitation was made, to attend relevant events such as case conferences and, in one case, a meeting of the Area Review Committee on Non-Accidental Injury.

(7) Interviews were held with key personnel from other agencies in the area, in particular with police officers with special responsibilities for juveniles and NSPCC personnel.

All the material was then collated into an 'Areabook' covering a standardised range of topics relevant to the project concerns.

Sample Surveys

In each local authority interviews were conducted with 30 social workers. The interview schedule was developed after two-stage piloting. Unstructured interviews were tape-recorded and content analysed. Semi-structured interview

6

schedules were developed and subsequently a more structured, but still relatively open-ended format was finalised. The interview usually took between 40 minutes and 75 minutes to complete and covered:
– background information (age, experience, qualifications);
– court experience (extent of experience, feelings about court);
– social enquiry reports (importance of and approach to);
– local authority solicitor (experience, perceptions and expectations of);
– courts officer (role of);
– solicitor representing children and parents (attitude to representation, contact with, attitudes, expectations, perceptions and stereotypes);
– police (contact with);
– changes and improvements to the system;
– attitudes to social work (professional status issues).

The intention had been to make a random selection of social workers (both qualified and unqualified) to interview from the area offices included in the study, excluding those with less than one year's experience and those who did not deal with children's cases. However in practice, given current vacancies, secondments, etc., this meant interviewing virtually all the social workers within the criteria. The total sample of social workers was 150.

In each local authority interviews were conducted with 10 private solicitors. Solicitors who had some experience of child care cases were identified from a number of sources; the cases included in the study, from local authority solicitors, courts officers, social workers, private solicitors, and where necessary, legal aid lists. In most areas all those operating in the area were interviewed. Individual solicitors were contacted direct and their cooperation sought. Only one solicitor contacted refused to be interviewed. The interview with solicitors concerned:
– background information (age, sex);
– organisation and work of the practice (size, work type, work organisation, specialisation);
– work of solicitor (specialisation, experience of care cases, advocacy, legal aid);
– role of solicitor representing the child (role perceptions, tasks, difficulties);
– role of solicitor representing the parents;
– pre-hearing contact with social workers and local authority solicitors (cooperation, nature of, difficulties in);
– social enquiry reports (attitudes to and expectations of);
– social workers and the law (perceptions of competence, attitudes to solicitors);
– court hearings (perceptions of, attitudes to);
– high court hearings;
– changes and improvements to the system.

On average the interview took one hour and a total of 50 interviews were conducted.

Sample of Cases

The study was concerned with the decision-making process in those cases which involved varying parental rights and recourse to the courts. Cases were

therefore included when the legal proceedings were of a number of different types:
- care proceedings under S.1(2) Children and Young Persons Act (CYPA) 1969 including proceedings brought by any relevant authority; and including applications to change a supervision order to a care order (S.15);
- criminal prosecutions brought by the police (when a care order was being recommended as a disposal option);
- applications by parents to vary or discharge a care order;
- wardship cases;
- S.2 Children Act (CA) 1948 resolutions in which parental consent was not obtained and the local authority needed to make an application to the juvenile court;
- variation of orders made under Matrimonial Causes Act (MCA) 1973 (i.e. when there was an existing custody order on a child and proceedings under this act were appropriate);

The following table shows the distribution of case types included in the study.

Table 1 Cases Included in the Study by Authority and Type of Case

Type of Proceedings	Local Authority					
	1	2	3	4	5	Total
Care Proceedings CYPA 1969						
S.1.2 a) proper development	2	8	5	5	3	23
b) same household	1	1	3	1	1	7
c) moral danger	1	1	–	–	1	3
d) beyond control	1	–	3	3	1	8
e) education	1	1	2	2	2	8
f) offence	–	–	–	–	–	–
Subtotal	6	11	13	11	8	49
Criminal Prosecutions	–	1	–	2	2	5
Discharge of a Care Order	1	1	1	1	1	5
Opposition to S.2 Resolution (CA 1948)	1	1	–	–	1	3
Wardship	4	1	1	1	1	8
Variations of orders under MCA 1973	2	–	–	–	–	2
Total	14	15	15	15	13	72

It was intended to study the progress of 15 cases in each local authority. Once the initial meetings had been conducted in an authority and contact made with relevant staff a system was established for identifying cases as they occurred. This system varied between authorities according to their structure but always involved liaison with the local authority solicitor and at least one member of each area office, (courts officers, area director, team leader, etc.). The research team also checked with staff at regular intervals. All cases which

were current in an area were studied until the target of 15 was reached. In the two urban authorities (1 and 5) the target was not reached despite contact being maintained over at least nine months (14 and 13 cases were obtained respectively). The time taken to achieve the sample depended on the frequency of cases and reflected the relevant case pattern of the various offices. Cases in which the social services were directly involved were readily identified. Cases brought by other agencies, particularly the education department or the police where the social worker was only involved in writing a report were less easily identified at an early stage. The distribution of cases obtained suggests that cases where care orders were made as a result of criminal prosecutions were under-represented in comparison with national figures. Repeated checks were made to ensure that these cases were not being missed. Criminal cases in which home circumstances reports were made by the probation service and where the social services were not involved would not have been included. In addition any instances of courts making a care order on a child as a recorded disposal in which a care order already was in force would not have been included.

Once a case had been identified, data was collected on the case from a number of sources and recorded on a standardised record sheet. The record sheet covered:
- background of the child (age, sex, family structure);
- home circumstances of the parent or guardian or other contenders for the care of the child (household composition, housing type);
- past legal history involving the child;
- any circumstances relating to the child or its family relevant to the care, behaviour or development of the child;
- the sequence of steps in the decision-making process (the dates, event types, personnel involved and content);
- the court hearing (type, grounds, representation, witnesses, outcome);
- placement of child before, during and as a result of the hearing;
- any subsequent action intended by the parties (appeals, etc.).

The principal sources of information used were social services files, court reports, interviews with social workers and observation of court hearings.

In as many cases as possible a member of the research team attended the court hearing. In a number of cases (7) there was no hearing because the applicant did not proceed with the case. In some cases it was not possible to attend a hearing: one clerk of court refused to allow members of the team to observe cases. Insufficient notice of hearings or clashes of dates made observation in some other cases impossible.

The main hearing was observed in 42/65 cases that went to court. In addition interim hearings were attended in a number of cases. When a hearing was not observed, as much detail about it as possible was obtained from someone who had been present, usually the local authority solicitor or social worker.

It was usually only possible to make brief notes in the courtroom. Full notes were made as soon as practicable after a hearing and subsequently written up. Standard information was recorded on the details of representation, people present, procedure, witnesses, main facts and arguments, and outcome. Observations were also made of the roles played and interactions between the

9

main participants both in and around the hearing. The time spent waiting for a case to be heard is one of the most important opportunities for direct contact between all the parties involved and particular attention was given to this period. To ensure that the members of the research team carrying out the observations maintained a shared conceptual approach, discussions and debriefing sessions were a feature of the project. Members also read each others fieldnotes and records. Whenever relevant, comments made on the hearings by solicitors and social workers were also recorded.

Analysis

Answers to all open-ended questions in the interview schedules were content analysed and a coding frame developed. The coding system sought to reflect the frame of reference of the respondents, as well as the conceptual concerns of the study. The main analytic task was therefore qualitative. Quantitative analysis was also performed of the coded material with frequency distributions being obtained for all questions. Combined indexes were constructed in relation to some issues from answers given to a range of questions. A limited variable set was analysed with reference to a number of independent variables. For the social worker sample these included local authority, sex, age, social work qualifications and experience, special court or legal experience, frequency of court experience. For the solicitor sample, local authority and specialisation were included. All differences were tested for significance (using mainly the Chi square test) and only when significant differences were found are they reported in the body of the text.

In reporting the findings of this study we have tried to minimize the inclusion of figures in the script and only report those figures which are of particular interest. The precise size of any frequency or percentage cannot be given undue weight since the samples were not a random selection of the population. In addition since many of the answer categories were based on coding spontaneously given responses, their exact relative frequency is misleading. Responses to closed-ended questions or those indexes on which all respondents were coded are given in detail. In the text we have adopted the convention of describing the relative frequency of responses, where actual figures are not given, as follows: large majority or most (75% +); majority (50 – 75%); a significant proportion (25 – 50%); some (10 – 25%); and a few (less than 10%).

In analysing the material from the cases we have tried to preserve a clear distinction between three types of data:
- factual material, e.g. the age of the child, the type of proceedings, whether or not a solicitor represented the parents;
- observations made by the research team or others in which a degree of subjectivity is likely to have been involved (e.g. behavioural problems of a child, roles played in court);
- interpretative assessments made of the case (e.g. adequacy of the case, conflict between parties).

All cases were analysed to produce a comparable set of material. Case records were subjected to a series of analyses in relation to a set of dependent and independent variables, all tested for significant differences.

10

Structure of report

To provide a background for the discussion of the roles played by social workers and solicitors and for the handling of cases Chapter II describes the relevant organisational system of each local authority highlighting important points of difference. In Chapter III the role perceptions of social workers and solicitors are considered and the role issues as they see them, both for themselves and each other, are discussed. This section is based on the interview material gathered in the sample surveys. In this context the role of the local authority solicitor and the role expectations which the other groups have of him are also considered. In Chapter IV the handling of cases is reported including the types of cases, the pre-hearing sequence and the hearings in court. In the final chapter the effects and outcomes of the system, the decision-making process, and the relationships between the groups are discussed and consideration given to system weakness and possible improvements.

Chapter II   The local authorities

In this chapter the five local authorities included in the study are described. A brief social/geographic description is given of each Authority to set the background, followed by a résumé of the organisation of the social services department particularly as it relates to handling child care cases. The pattern of children in care and coming into care, as well as the residential resources available in the Authority are described. Any special features of other agencies and inter-agency liaison are mentioned in so far as they contribute to the handling of children's cases.

Later in the report other features of the local system are described in greater detail:

- the organisational background of each local authority legal department is described in conjunction with the roles played by the solicitors in Chapter III;
- the differing practices in relation to courts officers and liaison with magistrates is covered in Chapter III as part of a discusssion of the support systems available to social workers in their dealings with the courts;
- the physical and procedural character of each of the juvenile courts is described in Chapter IV prior to considering the handling of individual cases;

Authority 1

Authority 1 is a London Borough which was created in its present form in 1965. The Borough is densely populated (0.2 million population in 0.02 million acres). The housing pattern is predominantly owner-occupation although there are a number of large council estates, some of which are high-rise. The Borough population has been declining. There has been a tendency for working age people to move out of central London and there has been a corresponding increase in the proportion of elderly and children in the population of the area. The part of the Borough nearest inner London is a transitional zone with the characteristic pattern of multiple house occupation, high mobility and settlements of immigrant groups. Further out there is a residential and commuter zone containing a green belt and affluent middle class area. The Borough is cut by a main arterial route along a river valley with concentrations of industrial and council housing developments. The Borough thus divides into four quarters: an inner middle class area; an outer middle class, green belt area; an inner industrial working class area with high-rise council housing; and an outer mixed industrial/residential area. The political geography follows this pattern both in the council and in parliamentary seats. As elected in 1978 the council has a Conservative majority.

The Social Services Department has four area offices divided on a geographical basis corresponding to the areas just described. All four areas were included in the study. The character of the work demands made on Social Services is rather different in the four areas. The child care problems are concentrated in the inner working class area. All four offices operated generic teams, and two had intake teams, at the time of the study.

The Social Services Department was experiencing staffing problems both centrally and in field work staff. Centrally the Department had a major administrative staff shortage: for example, the Department had no research staff, and there was one person acting as courts officer for the whole area as well as carrying responsibility for intermediate treatment. At field staff level there was thought to be high turnover of staff and difficulty in recruitment because of competition with neighbouring boroughs. In comparison with the other authorities in the study this Authority had a comparatively high proportion of inexperienced and unqualified staff.

The Borough has nine residential establishments for children with 136 places. This includes two residential nurseries and one former remand home which was being converted to an observation and assessment centre with some secure accommodation. There is considerable difficulty obtaining foster parents, particularly short-term placements, and it is not unusual for young children to be placed in residential nurseries, particularly when awaiting the outcome of court proceedings. (The statistics for the area show that a relatively low percentage of children in care are boarded out.) However the number of children in care, particularly those on care orders, is low in comparison with national figures (about 300). In a year about thirty children become subjects of care orders and about twelve S.2 resolutions are passed by the Social Services Committee. Social workers feel that the Authority has not given sufficient priority to intermediate treatment and prevention activities and there are relatively few schemes or facilities in operation.

All the area offices use one juvenile court just outside the Authority boundaries. (One area occasionally uses another court.) This is an extremely busy court and considerable operational difficulties occur (delays in getting court dates, long waiting periods, unsuitable facilities). The police operate a Juvenile Liaison Bureau in the area headed by a Superintendent. The Bureau appears to have good liaison with the Social Services Department particularly at senior level and in relation to non-accidental injury cases. Liaison with local police stations is more problematic for social work staff.

The Education Welfare Service in the area consults the Social Services Department on non-school attendance cases. If a care order is thought necessary, the responsibility for court proceedings may be handed over to the Social Services, although disagreement can occur on the merits of such proceedings.

The Borough has an active Area Review Committee (ARC) and a working party on NAI (non-accidental injury) which keeps procedure and problems under review. Since the committee meets relatively frequently (every 3 months) it serves an important liaison function for senior members of relevant agencies in the area. The Borough has access to the NSPCC National Advisory Centre for the Battered Child as a specialist resource. Members of the Centre take

part in the ARC, may attend case conferences, and are occasionally consulted by social workers, but it is not a major force in the handling of individual cases.

Authority 2

Authority 2 is a large, diverse non-metropolitan county in southern England. It covers half a million acres and has a population of 600,000. In the 1974 reorganisation some changes were made to the boundaries of the County but otherwise it remained unchanged. The County has a strip of coastal towns to the south with a significant retirement and holiday population. The proportion of the population over 65 in the county is relatively high. To the north the County is within reach of London and has large commuter areas, some of which are 'new town' in type. Geographically the bulk of the County is rural with agricultural areas interspersed with towns, which often operate as dormitory towns. The County in general has high housing standards and is relatively affluent, always returning Conservative members of parliament and electing a council with a large Conservative majority. The County is quite large and, although it has excellent train services on the commuter routes to London, transport can be difficult. The County follows the pattern of other rural areas in the south of England where the reduction in the agricultural labour force and the growth of the larger towns has created a pattern of the retreat of services away from the countryside into the towns. The headquarters of the Local Authority is in one corner of the County which creates travelling problems particularly to the London commuter area which lies at maximum distance from the Head Office.

The Social Services Department has eight area offices; five are located along the coastal fringe, one office is in the area on the edge of London, and two are in towns serving the rural hinterland. Three offices were included in the study; one coastal town, one rural area and the area close to London. The character and pattern of social services work differs in the three areas. All the areas have adopted the organisational structure of an intake team plus generic long-term teams. None have specific child care teams although the personal preferences of social workers have resulted in some teams having a family and child care emphasis. In the coastal area the greatest demand on the social services is made by the elderly, although cases with complex family problems do arise and holiday populations can also create special problems. The area near to London was settled by a relatively homogeneous population in the 1950's and the emphasis of social services demand is changing as the population ages. In the past the emphasis has been on children but now there is an increasing demand made by the elderly and by 'teenage tearaways' from broken homes or families where both parents are working. The ratio of children in care in these two areas is relatively high in comparison with the rural areas. The rural area, which includes a commuting 'stockbroker belt', has a mixed case load and the long-term work is mainly with problem families and with children covered by statutory orders.

The central structure of the Authority includes a County Coordinator for Child Care who acts as an advisor on child care and is available for consultation on complex cases. He chairs many case conferences as well as the Area

Review Committee on NAI, and maintains the risk register. He has played a particularly significant role in improving what had previously been poor relationships with the police in parts of the County.

The head office is well-supplied with support staff including research and training departments. The County currently has a well-qualified social work establishment and has introduced the senior practitioner grade as a means of providing promotion for fieldwork staff.

The Authority has 27 residential establishments for children with 302 places, including one residential nursery and five observation and assessment centres. The current policy emphasis is on fostering and home placements; the overall level of boarding out of children in care is higher than average and the number of children 'home-on-trial' has been rising. Young children are placed with foster parents except when there is a positive reason to place them in a nursery (e.g. after the breakdown of a foster placement). Previously the Authority had invested in family group homes but legislative changes affecting the staffing of the homes, the changing nature of demand, and staff turnover problems meant that this form of provision is no longer satisfactory. The emphasis on fostering is reflected in the decision to convert a hostel into a pre-fostering unit where families can be given support and preparation for fostering. In addition, a special scheme is in operation to try to attract foster parents for difficult teenagers.

The number of children in care has been steady in recent years at about 900, with around 100 children coming into care under care orders per year. The proportion of care orders made following criminal prosecutions is significantly lower than the national average (although it has been rising). This may be partly a reflection of the character of the area but may also be as a result of the police agreeing not to prosecute if the Social Services are prepared to take action on other grounds. The number of children in care on orders made under the Matrimonial Causes Act 1973 is relatively high in this Authority apparently as a result of the view of a judge who sits locally that proceedings involving children on custody orders should be heard by the matrimonial rather than the juvenile court. S.2 Resolutions are passed by a Parental Rights subcommittee of the Social Services Committee. The Education Welfare Service seems to play a minor role in bringing child care cases and are not represented on the Area Review Committee.

The County is administered in nine petty sessional divisions and there are ten court houses. Each of the three areas has a main juvenile court located in the same town as the Area Office. Occasionally cases are heard in courts in other areas sometimes because the child is placed there.

Authority 3

Authority 3 is a non-metropolitan county in eastern England which was formed in 1974 by the amalgamation of an administrative county and two county boroughs. It is a very large, mainly agricultural, county (1.3 million acres), with industrial centres in the county town and two medium-sized towns on the opposite edges of the County. The population is just over half a million. Depopulation has occurred in the rural areas and the County is both a holiday

and retirement area. There is a relatively high proportion of elderly people in the population and this has been recognised in a shift in policy priorities towards the elderly.

The geographical size of the County, difficulties in transport and the isolation of the rural communities are important features of the Authority. There are special problems in the provision of resources: centrally located resources such as the legal department are restricted in their services because of distance; residential homes and children's facilities may be located at considerable distance from families; intermediate treatment schemes are difficult to organise because of travelling problems. Local networks are influenced by family and personal relationships and the decision-making system is susceptible to public pressure and local concerns. The county town is an exception to this pattern as it is a large city with densely populated, deprived inner areas. The city has in the past been Labour controlled in contrast to the rest of the County, with a tradition of a high standard of social services provision. The 1974 amalgamation created integration problems and priority spending was shifted to the rural areas.

The Social Services Department is organised on a 3-region basis with a regional as well as a central management structure. There are 12 area offices, including 3 in the main city. The study was conducted in 4 areas; one inner city area which was organised on a specialist team basis with rotating responsibility for duty and intake; one area including a seaside/port town and two largely rural areas. The latter three areas all operated generic teams and work was distributed on a geographical-patch basis. The city area teams have all the demand problems of a decaying inner city area. In the seaside-port town there are particular problems with juvenile crime arising from seasonal employment and the influx of holiday-makers in the summer. There are a number of armed forces establishments in the rural areas and, on occasions these created special problems in child care.

The regional structure includes the management of children's resources including residential establishments, playgroups, childminders, fostering and IT. The Authority has 15 residential establishments providing about 290 places including 2 observation and assessment centres and one intermediate treatment centre. There is no residential nursery and young children are normally placed with foster parents, although there is difficulty finding sufficient foster parents particularly in the city area. There was no secure accommodation available at the time of the study. On average there are about 800 children in care with about 120 children coming into care under court orders in a year. S.2 resolutions are taken by the full Social Services Committee and an average of 30 are passed in a year.

The County is administered in 13 petty sessional divisions and there are 12 courts which can be used as juvenile courts, some only sitting when there is a sufficient case list. The city area has a busy court, sitting regularly with several courtrooms. A number of area offices use this court, including two in the study. In the port area there is one court sitting regularly, and there are two courts in the remaining area, each sitting monthly. In these two areas there is close personal contact between magistrates, solicitors and courts officers. There is also active co-operation with police.

The pattern of local authority legal services in this Authority is markedly different from the others in the study. The manning of the Department is inadequate for the demand and it is not uncommon for private solicitors to represent the local authority. In the city area there was a tradition of using private solicitors and the preference for doing so has remained. In the more distant areas the practicalities of travelling and a preference for working with a local man both create a trend towards private representation. Social workers therefore tend to know personally a small group of solicitors who have developed a speciality in child care work.

The County has an Area Review Committee on NAI and a printed procedural handbook. NAI case conferences are the responsibility of area officers and a structured format sheet is used for recording case conferences and their decisions. The Risk Register is maintained at County Hall. A senior police officer has responsibility for NAI cases and takes an active part in all such cases.

Authority 4

Authority 4 is a non-metropolitan county in the midlands formed in 1974 by the amalgamation of the county borough and administrative county. The County is moderately large (0.6 million acres) and has a population of around half a million. The area is largely rural in character with a number of well-established towns, a major county town and an industrial town which is suffering severe problems of industrial decline. Both major towns have development corporations and rebuilding programmes affecting the town centres and surrounding housing areas. The new estates in the county town have housed young families particularly from London and the proportion of young children in the population is relatively high. With the exception of the industrial town of the northern border of the county the standard of housing and availability of employment is comparatively good. Currently the Council is controlled by the Conservatives with a large majority, taking over from Labour in the 1977 elections and four out of five parliamentary constituencies are held by Conservatives.

The Social Services Department with its headquarters in the county town is divided into 7 geographical areas; 2 in the large towns, 2 in the smaller, older towns and 3 covering rather diffuse rural areas. The study included one area of each type. The county town area is large in population terms, effectively combining two areas, and is organised on a client-group basis. There are 3 teams which make up a child care section, managed by a deputy area officer. The deputy area officer takes specific responsibility for the decision to take care proceedings. The high case load of juvenile court cases justifies the maintenance of a court section with two nearly full-time officers. The members of this section have created a strong local liaison system with the courts, magistrates, solicitors, the police, and the legal department. The two other area offices are much smaller and have only a small number of child care cases in a year. One has an intake and long term team, the other operates an entirely generic system. Both areas have senior practitioners acting as specialists, including in child care, and a member of staff acting as courts officer. Local

liaison in relation to child care cases is much less developed than in the city. The Social Services Committee has accepted that social work field-staffing has not kept pace with demand and there are plans to increase the establishment and to protect the fieldwork services from cuts in expenditure.

A child placement unit is located in the Social Services Department head office structure. The Authority has 23 residential establishments for children providing 252 places but it is planned to close 2 of the 17 children's homes and the only residential nursery in response to expenditure cuts. There are 3 observation and assessment centres in the Authority area and a unit with secure accommodation will be opened soon. There is a lack of places for girls in community homes with education. It is anticipated by the Director of Social Services that the recommendations made to the courts for care orders may be affected in future by the unavailability of placements. Currently the policy of the placement unit is that recommendations should not be determined by availability of resources. The areas are able to place young children with foster parents, usually locally, and in general there is a move to increase adoption, fostering and 'home-on-trial' placements and to reduce residential placements.

There are about 950 children in the care of the Local Authority and 70 – 80 care orders made in any one year, nearly half of these following criminal prosecutions. Resolutions under S.2 1948 C.A. are relatively rare and are taken by the full Social Services Committee, or in between meetings by a quorum and later ratified. In the latter case the social worker attends to speak to the report, but does not if the resolution is taken in full committee. The resolution to be put is prepared by the legal department in consultation with the social worker.

There is (at least nominally) a liaison committee between Education and Social Services. However conflict does sometimes arise between departments over particular cases. The legal department has taken an active part in seeking to regulate liaison over cases. A procedure has been prepared emphasising the need for meetings between departments if the Education Department wishes to take legal action in respect of a child. If there is conflict between departments the legal department can convene a meeting and act in a mediating role.

The overall system for handling cases, particularly those involving possible non-accidental injury, is affected by the presence of a NSPCC Special Unit. The Unit was set up in this Authority in 1974 following a request of the Area Review Committee on NAI. It functions as a specialist service for the whole county and was responsible for developing the NAI handbook and procedural guidelines. The unit is responsible for running NAI case conferences, monitoring cases and maintaining the NAI register. It thus provides a systematic and coherent influence on some features of the decision-making and management of all NAI cases in the Authority. With many of its responsibilities delegated to the Special Unit the ARC only meets annually. The Unit also provides a casework, treatment and consultation service. The Head of the Unit is in close contact with members of the Area Review Committee and maintains an important liaison network with senior members of all related agencies. This authority-wide network can occasionally override the local systems and may significantly affect the progress of a case.

There are nine petty sessional divisions in the Authority area, each with a

courthouse. These are administered in four groups each with its own office and clerk. In the three areas in the study each social services area office was located in the same town as the juvenile court it used. The police in the Authority operate in four divisional areas with a woman police constable responsible for juvenile liaison in each division. In the county town the courts officer conducts personal discussions with the police on the handling of juveniles but in the other areas the liaison is largely confined to formal notification of police action. A Chief Inspector at headquarters has particular responsibility for children and domestic violence. The Chief Constable is a member of the ARC. Police are always included in case conferences in NAI cases and actively involved in decision-making in these cases.

Authority 5

Authority 5 is a densely populated (300,000 population), industrial urban area in the mid to north west of England. As a metropolitan borough it is the result of the 1974 amalgamation of a county borough and parts of other authorities. As an administrative unit it is therefore comparatively new. It is relatively small in geographical area (0.02 million acres) and includes a number of old mining towns which have developed into a continuous urban sprawl. Despite serving as a suburban area for the neighbouring metropolis, there remains a relatively strong community structure based on the old towns. The area is industrially active and unemployment is not a major problem. The population is growing rapidly. There is a relatively low proportion of vulnerable groups. The main problem areas for Social Services are a number of rather isolated and poorly serviced council estates. The Authority has a large proportion of council housing and owner-occupied houses. The council has a Conservative majority.

The Social Services Department has five relatively small area offices (all included in the study). Each area has a somewhat different organisation based either on an intake/generic long term team structure, or a specialist teams structure (three areas have child care teams).

A Principal Social Worker has responsibility for specialist child care services for the Authority including adoption, fostering, intermediate treatment, care cases, and maintaining the Risk Register. Also based centrally there is a courts officer section with two full time officers. The local authority solicitor, located nearby, has a close identification with all social services work. The courts officers, the solicitor and the Principal Social Worker work together: a courts officer attends all cases and co-operates with the solicitor; the solicitor and the Principal Social Worker also work together and both attend case conferences. In addition the courts officers have a well-developed liaison system with the police which includes weekly meetings to discuss action on juveniles. Fieldworker representatives also attend weekly juvenile cautioning sessions run by the police. Some areas also have contact with the local 'residential beat officers' but the more distant offices are somewhat deprived of localised police contacts by the operation of the central system. The centralised system services all five areas and courts and introduces a coherent organisational pattern in the handling of cases throughout the Authority.

The area is served by six community homes with 78 places. It has no residential nursery and until recently has had to use observation and assessment facilities in a neighbouring Authority. There is a general policy of placing young children with foster parents and the Authority has sufficient placements to draw on. The Authority has about 450 children in care and about 60 children are made the subject of care orders in a year. S.2 resolutions 1948 C.A. are taken by the full Social Services Committee with the Director of Social Services and local authority solicitor attending. A sub-committee can also meet to deal with emergencies. On average, 17 resolutions are passed a year.

All non-school attendance cases are brought by the Education Department without involving the local authority solicitor. Centrally there are monthly liaison meetings between the Social Services and Education departments. Locally liaison varies and on occasions tensions can arise, for example, when social workers are not informed that proceedings are being taken.

The area is covered by three petty sessional divisions each with a juvenile court, two of the courts being administered by the same chief clerk. Three of the area teams use the main central court which meets twice weekly. The other two areas each use the court in the town and the procedural character and style of these courts differs markedly from the central court.

The Area Review Committee for the Authority is comprised of members of all the relevant agencies. It meets quarterly and takes an active interest in both the overall pattern of cases and the outcome of particular cases. The ARC prepared procedural guidelines for NAI cases and deals with any problems which arise in the operation of these procedures.

Chapter III Roles and role relationships of solicitors and social workers

This chapter examines the roles and role relationships of social workers, local authority solicitors and private solicitors, based on material drawn from interviews and discussions with solicitors and social workers in the 5 areas.

However, before introducing and discussing the views of social workers and solicitors on their roles it is important to record several significant features of the decision-making system involved in child care cases. First, it should be noted that the decision-making process is multi-stage and makes different role demands at each stage. Second, the decision-making process in relation to child care cases is only intermittently invoked and then often under crisis conditions. Third, the decision-making process involves some of the main participants in tasks and relationships which are different from those which are characteristic of their normal work.

The decision-making process in child care cases can be seen as being comprised of a number of different phases. These phases can be clearly distinguished analytically although in individual cases the phases are often confused, may occur concurrently and frequently involve recursive decision sequences which confuse the pattern. Each phase implies different tasks to be done and positions to be taken by the participants. Although the governing rules of the system place some restrictions on the way tasks and positions are defined in role terms, there is considerable flexibility in how the role definitions can develop.

Phase 1: Information Collection

Prior to taking a decision on care proceedings a base of information is prepared about the child, the family and significant events. If the family is known to the social services this information is usually contained in the social work file but needs to be extracted and collated. If the family is not known, or there has been a significant event, such as injuries to the child, information is gathered from a number of sources. If a number of agencies have had contact with the family, information from each is collected and shared.

Phase 2: Decision to Proceed

The decision to take proceedings can be seen as having four major elements:

(a) *The need for intervention*. Before deciding to take care proceedings it must be established that there is a need to intervene. The need may be defined by the circumstances of the child (for example, the need for the physical care or for protection from harm) or by externally defined criteria (failure to attend school, criminal activity).

21

(b) *Plans for the child*. In deciding to take care proceedings rather than some other action there should be a consideration of what would be done with the child, both in the short and the longer term, after obtaining a court order. This may include an assessment of available resources, appropriate placements and the likelihood of rehabilitation.

Depending on the type of case, (a) and (b) will carry different weight. If the need for intervention is sufficiently strong, as when a child has been non-accidentally injured, the decision to take care proceedings may be made whether or not there has been planning of the child's future. In other cases, particularly in non-school attendance cases, no decision may be taken unless a satisfactory placement is available, irrespective of the need factor.

(c) *Contingencies*. Since the circumstances relating to a family may change during the period before a care order can be obtained, the decision to take proceedings may be contingent on certain developments, for example, whether the child does attend school in the intervening period, the presence in the household of the person suspected of having injured the child, the outcome of criminal prosecutions by the police, etc.

(d) *The legal case*. A decision to take care proceedings may depend on whether the information available constitutes an adequate case to be presented to the court under the terms of the Act. The grounds under which the proceedings will be taken must be specified and the information relevant to proving those grounds and the availability of witnesses to testify must all be taken into account. Alternative procedures such as wardship and S.2 resolutions may also be considered.

Phase 3: Implementation

Three interlocking sets of activity follow from the decision to take a case to court:

(a) *Information gathering*. Depending on the adequacy of the original information available on the case, further information is gathered and the situation of the family is monitored over the intervening period. If contingencies were specified the decision may be reviewed and revised.

(b) *Placement, planning and management*. If the child was removed from home, his placement is managed and monitored prior to the case coming to court and plans are made for his future placement following the court hearing.

(d) *Case preparation*. The case is prepared for court and administrative steps are taken such as obtaining court dates, notifying the relevant parties, and making arrangements concerning representation. Information is collated and organised to form a case. Witnesses are obtained, proofs of evidence and reports are prepared and collected.

Phase 4: Decision

In the final phase of the decision process the case is heard in court; it is presented, witnesses are examined and cross-examined and professional reports and evidence are given.

The extent to which these stages occur and are clearly separable from each other will vary according to the nature of the case. For example, in a case of suspected non-accidental injury in relation to a family not previously known to the social services, the information and decision phase may all be encapsulated within a case conference called specially for the purpose. (In a well-run case conference of this type each element will be clearly specified and recorded in the case conference record.) In a case which is well-known to the social services and involving a family with whom the social worker has worked for many years, the decision to take proceedings may evolve gradually, depending upon a variety of contingencies which are poorly specified and often not recorded. In some cases the stages may be reiterated several times. If the information available is not thought adequate to prove a case in the juvenile court, the decision to take proceedings may be reviewed on a number of occasions as the situation of the family changes. At some stage a decision may be made not to go ahead with proceedings and the sequence may then be truncated.

The above sequence of stages has been described in relation to the decision to take care proceedings, but similar stages are also involved if the alternative procedures of S.2 resolution or wardship are involved. In the case of a S.2 resolution the full sequence involving a court hearing only occurs if the parents are opposed to the resolution being passed. In principle a similar series of stages is also involved in the decision to revoke a care order, even if the initiative in this case comes from the parents making the application.

Each stage of the process described above implies sets of tasks to be done and roles to be played. For a particular individual his roles may vary from one step to another. The social worker is likely to be involved in each stage of the process and may perform a number of roles. He may act as the caseworker and resource manager in relation to the child and the family and as such may be an important witness in the case when it comes to court. He may act as the agency representative in relation to the decision to take proceedings either taking the decision himself, as a member of a group or accepting the decision made by someone else. He may play a management role in relation to the case, organising and coordinating people and information. As the social work professional he may act as advisor to the court, preparing a report on the child and its family and making recommendations.

Solicitors are less likely to be involved in all stages in the process and it is an important role issue as to how far they should be involved. For example, should the local authority solicitor take part in the decision phase or only in case preparation? Even when solicitors clearly have a part to play, as in the presentation of the case in court, the nature of the role, its proper tasks and responsibilities, is uncertain. This is particularly problematic for a solicitor representing the child.

Potentially the multi-stage nature of the decision-making process creates a range of role problems for both social workers and solicitors including problems of role definition, role shift and role conflict. In general the development of clear and shared role definitions depend on individuals having opportunities to experience the difficulties and practice solutions. However the opportunities to explore the role issues involved in bringing child care cases to court are fairly limited both for social workers and solicitors since the system is only

invoked sporadically and often under emergency conditions.

Children taken into care under statutory orders comprise a relatively small proportion of all children taken into care during the year (75% of all children taken into care in a year are received into care on a voluntary basis). Although there is considerable variation between area offices, the average number of care orders made in a year for any given office is about ten. In a large city authority, the number of care orders may be significantly higher than 10, whereas in small rural areas there may be only one or two care orders made in any year. Most social workers have therefore relatively little first-hand experience of the roles and procedures involved in care proceedings. In addition the concept of generic social work requires social workers to maintain a general competence in many fields other than those relating to care proceedings.

For private solicitors, too care proceedings occur relatively infrequently in their overall case load. Only about a quarter of the solicitors interviewed handled more than 15 child care cases a year and the average was about 10. The local authority solicitors on the other hand have more continuous contact with this type of case than any of the other parties, usually spending 50% or more of their time on child care work.

When a system is operated regularly the participants have opportunities to learn about their respective roles and responsibilities, and to develop role management skills. When a system is only operated intermittently, and then often under crisis conditions, role uncertainty and lack of shared role concepts can be significant role issues. When people operate under role uncertainty they are vulnerable to inefficiency, either because tasks are not completed or there is redundancy in the completion of tasks. Disagreements and tensions may also arise because there is no agreement about who is responsible for what and excessive time may have to be spent in coordination.

Over and above the role uncertainty concerned with the allocation of tasks, the operation of a complex inter-agency network such as that involved in care proceedings raises problems in relation to the cooperation and trust necessary for efficient communication. Where decisions must be made under time pressures there is never sufficient opportunity to spell out every detail in a communication between two people. Certain elements must be taken for granted and trust must exist that information passed between people will not be used for inappropriate purposes. In particular there must be agreement between the parties as to the status and confidentiality of information transmitted. When an inter-agency network is only invoked intermittently the opportunity to develop understanding and trust will be limited. Failures of communications, misunderstandings and conflict about inappropriate communications can be expected under these circumstances. It is not therefore surprising that breakdowns of communications are a feature of those cases which have received so much publicity at either national or local level.

A third feature of the system which has important role implications is that it involves the participants in activities which are different in type from those which they normally perform. For a social worker working with families and children the decision to initiate care proceedings involves a significant change in his mode of relating to the client. Social case-work philosophy is concerned

with working in cooperation with and with the agreement of the client, supporting the client to enable him to be self-managing and independent, providing a professional service and access to agency services. Social workers try to manage receptions into care (Section 1, 1948 Children Act) within this framework. Even the assumption of Parental Rights under Section 2 may be seen as consistent with the case work philosophy, since the agreement of parents is actively sought and usually obtained. However, in care proceedings the social worker acts as an agent of the state seeking powers over a child. Except where the parents agree that the child is beyond their control the decision is usually opposed in some way by the client. In assuming the power to remove the child from its parents, the social worker is usually acting to divide the family and not to assist in its maintaining itself as a unit.

Private solicitors may also be required to change their mode of operation and their relationships with their clients in care proceedings. For example, the solicitor normally seeks to carry out the wishes of the person who approaches him, namely his client. If a parent approaches him in relation to care proceedings he may only be able to act for the child and his relationship with the parent is ambiguous.

Where people are required to perform roles from time to time which involve significant shifts in tasks and relationships they are likely to experience conflict. If the nature of the conflict is not clearly understood, these difficulties may create anxiety. Undoubtedly an element in the anxiety reported by social workers in relation to care proceedings is created by the seriousness of cases of this type. But role conflict also contributes significantly to this unease.

In summary, the decision-making process in child care cases is multi-stage; it is used only intermittently; it is often begun under crisis conditions; and involves some of the main participants in tasks and relationships which are different from those in their normal work. Since it is a system which has many participants it is likely to raise a range of role issues; proper role definition, handling multiple roles, role boundaries, role co-ordination and role conflict.

Social workers' views of role issues

Social workers do not feel that they have enough knowledge of the law relating to child care; only 21% of the sample thought that they had sufficient training in this area. A larger proportion of those people working in teams which concentrate on child care are more confident of their knowledge base (41%). However the overall level of experience, qualifications or experience of court do not appear to contribute to a feeling of having adequate preparation. When asked what steps they thought they would need to take if they had a case which might involve legal proceedings, 88% said that they would contact the local authority solicitor, or discuss the matter with their senior (47%), but very few had specific ideas about the kinds of tasks which might be involved; 23 mentioned calling a case conference, 29 advising the client on legal representation, 19 contacting relevant agencies and 15 administrative steps such as sending out notices. This does not imply that social workers would not

know what to do in care proceedings. It does however indicate that they do not have a conscious procedural model of care proceedings which they can describe. Both the reported lack of training in the law and the inability to articulate specific tasks associated with taking care proceedings indicate that social workers experience a degree of uncertainty in this area of work.

In the exploratory phase of the study we found that social workers expressed their views about care proceedings in talking about 'the court'. The court is a natural focus of attitudes to care proceedings since the court hearing is the event around which activities are organised and in which all the dynamics of the case are played out in public. Social workers experience the courts not only in care proceedings but also in relation to criminal prosecutions, particularly those concerning children who are already in care. There is considerable variation between social workers in the extent of their court experience; 35% said they had a lot of experience of court work, 41% quite a bit, and 24% not much or none. A somewhat better indication of the frequency with which social workers go to court is given by the estimates of how often they had been to court in the last twelve months; 33% said they had been less than four times in the previous year, 27% between five and ten times and 39% had been to court on more than eleven occasions. The median frequency is once every two months. By virtue of carrying particular roles or from past experience some social workers have a particular knowledge of the court: past or present court officers (11); previous experience as policemen (3), probation officers (8), lawyers (2), or ex-child care officers (15). Some social workers expressed positive attitudes to the court saying that they enjoy going to court, they like the experience, or they find it interesting (19%) and another 43% are fairly neutral in their attitudes. However, 32% of social workers express negative feelings about the court, saying that it makes them nervous, anxious and that they don't like the experience. A small group expressed extremely negative attitudes saying that they found the court frightening and they hated it.

Experience of court is clearly an important factor in a social worker's attitude to court. Most of those expressing positive attitudes to the court said that they had a lot of court experience, whereas the negative attitudes were largely expressed by young social workers, unqualified social workers and those with very little court experience. However experience of court does not completely explain the social workers' attitudes since there are a significant number with a considerable amount of court experience who still express negative attitudes. Since courts vary widely in their physical and social character, attitudes to court might be determined by the nature of the local juvenile court. However, analysis of the data shows that this is not the case. Since neither the character of the court nor experience of the court environment fully explain social workers' negative feelings, some other factors must be operating.

One element in the social workers attitude to the court seems to be a response to the court as an unfamiliar and strange environment. Anyone attending a busy magistrates court is often appalled by its social organisation. To those who are familar with the organisation of a modern, bureaucratic institution, the court appears at once chaotic and outmodedly formal, authoritarian and secretive. Social workers describe their experience of court

in terms of feeling uncertain of what to do, what was happening and who people were. Many felt that the court staff and information systems gave them no guidance or help. Some also perceived the court as chaotic and disorganised.

The social worker normally functions in an organisation system in which roles and role relationships are defined and impersonalised; where there is a formal information storage and retrieval system (e.g. centralised filing and record keeping systems); decisions are mainly made by consensus and compromise (e.g. case conferences); and there is a clear boundary between officials of the organisation and the public. Courts on the other hand have a different organisational form; they are a locus in which people from many places gather to do business within the constraints of established rules. The roles played are defined by the procedures, are only temporarily held and externally defined role status is not acknowledged. The information system is unsystematic and highly personalised. Decision-making is conducted in an adverserial win or lose manner. There is no clear distinction between members of the organisation and the public, except that which evolves socially between those who are and those who are not familiar with the courts.

Some social workers commented on the social boundaries operating in and around the court saying that they felt excluded, not a member of the in-group and that their presence was begrudged and their professional status not acknowledged. In contrast, those few social workers who had become really familiar with the court and members of the 'in-group' felt that the court atmosphere was friendly and welcoming.

Social workers expressed their attitudes to the court both in relation to their reactions to going to court and to aspects of the system they would like to see changed. Formality of the physical environment, in particular the formal layout and furniture of the courts, the magistrate sitting on a raised platform at some distance from other participants and the largeness of some courtrooms were mentioned by 53% of social workers at some point in their interviews. Formality of procedure and style were commented on by 64% of social workers; in particular, the impersonal style, the emphasis on dress, manners, etiquette and procedure. The inefficiency and disorganisation of court were commented on by 26% of social workers, particularly mentioning time wasted waiting for hearings, the time available for hearings and delays for adjournment.

While the negative feelings of anxiety and uncertainty associated with courts are for some people lessened as they become familiar with the courts, the more specific criticisms are not less common amongst experienced social workers. In fact those social workers with a great deal of court experience are more concerned about the formality of the physical setting of the court than others. The nature of the comments made suggests that in general social workers see courts as old-fashioned and disorganised in comparison with the bureaucratic environment with which they are familiar.

Changes in physical environment are often associated with changes in role, for example, the husband or wife role is played in the home and the employee role at the workplace. The association between physical environment and role can be so strong that the environment itself triggers the role change. Attempts

to play a role in its wrong physical setting can give rise to discomfort and embarrassment. When a man's family visits his place of work he may find this experience difficult although he may not be aware of the reason for his unease. This dynamic may contribute to the feelings of tension and uncertainty reported by even experienced social workers about going to court. In general however social workers do not spontaneously mention the role changes and role conflicts associated with going to court and only 5 people commented directly on this aspect.

Although social workers did not tend to discuss the role conflict between acting as a professional social worker and as a representative of the local authority, as arising particularly in care proceedings, most social workers did experience such tensions in the course of their work (83%). Resources were a major area on which such conficts occur; 51% mentioned the inadequacy and alllocation of resources, such as manpower, time, activities, tools, and physical resources. The second area in which conflict arises is in organisational matters: 46% mentioned tensions arising over paperwork, procedures, having to implement policies or decisions made by seniors or at council level, the tendency of the organisation to play safe and avoid publicity.

These issues can all be raised by care proceedings but these cases seem not to be separately identified by social workers as creating special problems. Perhaps the most overt form of these conflicts arises when the social worker does not agree with the decision to take care proceedings at all: 40% of social workers interviewed thought that there were cases in which the case should not have been taken to court. Since the social worker is usually a major participant in the decision-making process when cases are being brought by the social services department, these cases are largely those involving other agencies (principally the police bringing cases on trivial offences 59%). However, a few social workers also felt that there were instances in which the local authority acted out of fear of publicity and over-estimated the risks to the child.

Social workers recognise that conflicts between their professional and agency roles do occur in general. Indeed much of the debate concerning whether or not social work is a profession can be seen as a response to the tensions between these roles. (For a fuller discussion see Hilgendorf, 1978). Relatively few are explicitly aware of the issues of multiplicity of roles and role conflicts in relation to care proceedings unless they have been involved in a case which has brought out overt role conflicts. The failure to conceptualise the role issues in care proceedings is at least partly a result of not giving the matter attention, either during training or subsequently. We found that when these issues were discussed with groups of social workers at the conclusion of field work they confirmed that there were issues which they had never openly discussed and that such discussions could be useful. However the uncertainties which underlie social workers' attitudes to the court and the persistent feelings of being inadequately prepared in the law are perhaps more problematic and may require appropriate support systems to be overcome.

Specialists and support systems for social workers

When an organisation is called upon to carry out a function which constitutes

a comparatively small part of its overall work, but which demands special knowledge and skills, there are a range of strategies which can be adopted. The most common approach is to separate the function by the creation of specialist departments or posts. If the function concerned is self-contained and unconnected with other functions carried out by the organisation, this approach can be successful. When the specialist function is not an integral part of the wider organisational activities, specialisation can create a number of problems.

(a) Difficulties may arise in maintaining communication and cooperation between the specialists and other staff. Extra time and energy will be spent on coordination activities and it may become necessary to appoint supervisory staff to oversee the relationships between the specialists and the rest of the organisation.

(b) The organisational form creates artificial divisions in tasks and responsibilities and may lead to inefficiency, redundancy or other failures in service to customers.

(c) Specialisation leads to the deskilling of the staff from whom the tasks are removed; the deskilling process is difficult to contain and may reach a stage where the knowledge of the general staff is insufficient for them to realise the problems for which the specialist department exists or to know when to seek their help.

These kinds of problems were recognised in the decision to move towards generic social work. Even though some specialisation has been reintroduced (see organisational structure of area teams in Chapter II) there is general agreement that field social work staff must be able to relate to the whole range of their clients' needs. In this context the possibility of statutory intervention to assume the care and control of the child is seen as one of a range of options open to a social worker. It is not seen as a specialist function which can be hived off in a department or role.

If the specialisation strategy is not appropriate then other actions can be considered.

1. Procedures, Guides, Manuals

When a function is only occasionally carried out there is insufficient opportunity for operating staff to learn what to do first-hand. Special attention can be given to these tasks and clearly specified procedures and guidelines can be developed. To be successful, these guidelines should be prepared by those with special knowledge but translated into the non-specialist's frame of reference. They should give particular attention to the circumstances in which the procedures should be invoked and to points indicating the need of specialist help.

The procedural guides which have been developed in relation to non-accidental injury cases are a good example of procedures of this kind. All five local authorities had clear and well thought out guides on the action to be taken if the social worker (and all other related professionals) suspected that a child had been injured non-accidentally.

One of the five authorities had a form to be completed in all cases in which legal proceedings were being considered by the social work staff. This form was designed as a means of notifying the local authority legal department about cases. But it was laid out in such a way as to bring to the social workers' attention tasks and information appropriate to the proceedings which he may not have realised were necessary, for example, who would be a relevant witness and whether that witness would be prepared to give evidence.

At least one authority had produced an overall guide to legal proceedings involving children. While this guide was an excellent résumé of the law in the area it was not couched in either the language or frame of most operating social workers.

Guides and manuals have one major drawback: they must be freely and readily available and may need to be updated. Despite the excellence of the non-accidental injury procedural handbooks, we found that in many social work offices copies were not available and sometimes the booklets were out of print.

From observation and discussion it seemed to us that people generally underestimate the need for a high level of redundancy in the output of information in this area. One publication in one format used at one point in time will reach only a limited part of the target audience. If it is really the intention to inform social workers about procedures and practices then there should be a variety of material available in different forms and repeatedly issued to cope with turnover of staff. This would also be true for the wider area of knowledge of the law relating to children and the functioning of the courts. (For example, the CCETSW paper on Social Workers and the Courts (1974) was useful in its time but is now largely unknown and unavailable.)

2. Meetings, Courses, Training

Awareness of the issues involved in the specialist area and relevant knowledge can be developed by periodic events which concentrate on the topic. Intensive training courses can be designed to convey appropriate knowledge or develop relevant skills. Such courses can be useful for those with a particular interest in the area but maybe less useful in reaching a large body of operating staff. Shorter courses or regular meetings on the other hand can be effective in bringing the area to the attention of large numbers of staff.

There appear to be remarkably few specialist courses available for social workers in the legal aspects of child care. Short courses, seminars, discussion meetings, lectures, etc. are occasionally organised. The courses which were most highly thought of by social workers and most frequently requested, were those run in conjunction with local juvenile courts. In two of the areas studied, 2 – 3 day courses involving discussion and role playing had been organised by the court personnel in association with the social services department. Social workers who had attended these courses were very enthusiastic about them. The courses were run locally which also served the purpose of familiarising the social workers with the court setting and personnel. The disadvantage of the local basis of this development is that it depends upon the initiative and cooperation of local courts and tends to be insufficiently frequent to keep up with the turnover of social work staff.

Attendance at court hearings to observe cases is also a useful training exercise for social workers and some area offices have developed this practice. Others, however, are not in favour of the social workers using their time in this way. Although observing hearings can be extremely helpful particularly to new social workers, it is undesirable for juvenile court hearings to be overloaded with people who are not related to the case and some clerks of court will not allow any observers to be present.

In most of the areas included in the study meetings were held between social workers and members of the juvenile bench. These meetings sometimes began at the request of the magistrates. Social workers are generally in favour of such meetings finding it helpful to meet and discuss issues with the magistrates before whom they appear. Although called for another purpose they also serve a training function by bringing the area of proceedings in the court into focus. Since magistrates are part of the judiciary and social workers part of the executive these meetings may raise questions of independence. In areas where they do not occur it is usually because the clerk of the court is opposed to them on grounds of potential collusion. A few social workers also raised this issue and felt that their clients would come to question the independence of the court if they knew such meetings took place.

The organisation of meetings with magistrates varies from one area to another:

(a) Frequency; twice a year is most common, some meet three or four times a year.

(b) Membership; magistrates who sit in the juvenile court attend; the clerk sometimes attends but not always; some are restricted to senior social work staff and some are open to all social workers.

(c) Topics; the contents and type of meeting varies. In some instances social workers provide feedback on what has happened on cases which have come before the court. In others there is a topic for discussion or a paper given. One group functions more as a working group where issues currently of concern are discussed (e.g. the working of compensation orders.)

3. Consultancy or Special Responsibility Roles

Rather than separating the entire function for doing the specialised tasks, an individual or post can be nominated as a locus of knowledge and skills to be a resource for other staff. This role may carry monitoring or special coordination responsibilities. It may also be convenient to locate special tasks in this role. In relation to care proceedings the development of the courts officer role is an example of this approach. In two of the local authorities included in the study a child care adviser role is included in the central management structure. The specialist function of the courts officer will be described in some detail as this is a support system which directly addresses the problem of social workers' relation to the courts.

The courts officer role is organised differently in the various local authorities included in the study.

31

(a) Centralised role. In Authority 5 there is a court section located in the head office with full-time courts officers, each covering about half of the Authority area. In the London Borough (Authority 1) there is one courts officer located at head office who also has an overall responsibility for intermediate treatment. These two authorities, being comparatively compact geographically, can be served in this centralised way.

(b) Area office based courts officer. Six area offices (including all three Authority 4 areas, two in Authority 2 and one in Authority 3) had courts officers located in the area offices. However there was considerable variation in the organisation of these roles, for example, one area has a court section with two courts officers on nearly a full time basis. The amount of time spent by courts officers in other areas varies but they are mostly operating social workers carrying additional responsibility for the court work.

(c) No courts officer. Three of the areas had no courts officer role.

The development of the courts officer role is to some extent a reflection of the amount of court work which is involved but it also seems to depend on the importance placed on court work by the areas and the interest and skills of the person occupying the role.

Nearly all social workers thought that it was helpful to have a courts officer. They were asked what they saw as the function of the courts officer and a range of functions and tasks were mentioned.

(a) Administration and coordination of court work, including the organisation, collection and delivery of reports and documents, both to and from the court and the clarification of any confusion arising about the courts' decisions. 41% of social workers mentioned this aspect of the courts officer role and all courts officers see this as an important and in some cases sole function. In carrying out these routine administrative tasks the courts officer is acting as a specialist removing the responsibility for those tasks from the social workers. In some cases the courts officer attending court as a matter of routine may obviate the need for social workers to attend the court at all.

(b) Intermediary between the social workers and court. The courts officer may assist and advise social workers about procedural and administrative matters in relation to the court, such as timing, court numbers, etc. 46% of social workers saw this as a function of the courts officer.

(c) Advisory/teaching role. The courts officer can act as a resource of knowledge and skills on the court, the law, and procedures in relation to child care cases. 43% of social workers saw this as a part of the function of the courts officer. The courts officers who operated the role on a full, or nearly full-time basis, or who had special knowledge of the courts or law for other reasons, saw this as an important part of the function. However where the courts officer was simply an operating social worker who had been given this additional responsibility they did not see their role as including being a knowledge resource. Those who thought they

should act in this way expressed some reservations as to whether social workers were in fact able or prepared to use them as consultants or resource people. They were usually able to give instances where social workers had failed to consult them on cases where they felt they should have been consulted.

(d) Continuity of relationships with the court. The courts officer role was sometimes initiated after concern had been expressed by magistrates that they never got to know the social workers who appeared in court before them. The courts officer attending court on a regular basis can provide continuity, somebody who the magistrates know and trust. 40% of social workers recognised this aspect of the courts officer role. Most active courts officers also recognised that this was a significant aspect of their function.

(e) Representation of the social services department. As the person appearing in court regularly and known to the magistrates, the courts officer tends to be seen as the person who can deal with any matters arising from cases which concern the social services department. For example, he can deal with cases which were not previously known to the department; he can stand in when the social worker cannot attend; occasionally he can present the case when the local authority solicitor is not available; he may make arrangements regarding the presence and representation of clients; he may answer questions about the availability of resources. 48% of social workers saw this as a function of the courts officer. The most active and interested courts officers also saw this as an important part of their role. When this aspect of the role is most fully developed the courts officer becomes very actively involved in court organisation and relating to court staff and becomes indispensible to the smooth running and organisation of cases.

The role of courts officer as conceived of by the role holder in a particular area is not always consonant with the views of the social workers in that area. Overall, most courts officers see an important part of their function as maintaining liaison with local police and establishing close and cooperative relationships particularly in relation to the decision to caution or prosecute children. This rather specialised function is one of which many social workers are unaware.

In three of the Authorities there are additional specialist roles. In Authority 2 there is a Child Care Adviser located at the headquarters of the Authority who advises on the full range of child care matters, acts as a resource to social workers on child care law and procedure and who takes an active part in chairing and organising case conferences. In Authority 5 there is a Principal Social Worker (children), also located centrally with overall responsibility for such matters as care proceedings, adoption, fostering, intermediate treatment, maintaining the risk register and case conferences. In Authority 4 there is an NSPCC Special Unit which takes an active role in relation to non-accidental injury cases and is responsible for coordinating and often chairing case conferences and maintaining the risk register. In all three cases these roles have been important in introducing some standardisation in the running and recording of case conferences.

In view of the role uncertainties expressed by social workers in relation to care proceedings, their relative lack of experience in handling such cases and the infrequency of this contact, the support systems which are currently available are often inadequate. In areas with a high incidence of cases local awareness of the problem has led to the development of appropriate systems. However it is in those areas where social workers have least experience of cases that there is least available support. For this reason leaving development to occur at area level is probably insufficient and some provision may need to be made centrally, for example, in the provision of courses and procedural mechanisms.

The local authority solicitor

In preparing and presenting a case for court the social services department calls on legal services provided by the local authority. The legal department is usually located in the head office of the authority in the department of the county secretary or chief executive. The department provides all legal services including advisory services, servicing committees and handling litigation. As a specialist area of work, cases for the social services department are usually handled by one or two solicitors who deal with all child care cases in the authority and relate to all area social work offices.

In the past, child care officers took at least some cases to court without legal assistance. With the loss of specialists, the growing complexity of the law and the increasing practice of children and parents being represented, local authority solicitors are now involved in cases as a matter of course. It is, however, still the practice in some authorities for education welfare officers to take care proceedings on the grounds of non-school attendance without being legally represented.

Local authority legal departments have some important characteristics in common. Court work is handled by solicitors at assistant solicitor or senior assistant solicitor level, with some grading of work type according to complexity. There is only limited promotion available within the litigation department. Promotion within the local authority involves moving away from purely legal work to managerial jobs either as head of department or servicing the committees of the council, and ultimately to county secretary or chief executive level. The fairly small number of posts available in any one authority means that promotion is usually dependent on moving to another authority. This structure results in a fairly rapid turnover of solicitors providing services to social workers; perhaps an average stay of three years. Solicitors in these posts also tend to be fairly young and at the beginning of their careers although they may have had experience in private practice. All the solicitors handling child care cases in the five local authorities were in their late 20's to mid thirties.

Beyond these similarities, legal departments differ in their professional establishments, degree of administrative support and organisational structure. The inter-departmental relationships between the legal department and the social services department also vary, both at a structural level and in terms of

the allocation of tasks between social workers and solicitors. The role played by a solicitor in child care cases is to some extent constrained by these organisational considerations. However there is also scope for individual preference and style.

From discussions with solicitors and social workers about the role of solicitors and observations of the roles being operated in practice we have identified three contrasting types of role definition:

1. *Legal consultant.* The legal consultant advises on details of the law, assists in complicated cases, and may give an opinion on the likelihood of the case succeeding in court.

2. *Social Work Advocate.* The advocate takes an active part in case preparation, advises on the sufficiency, strengths and weaknesses of evidence, and acts as the social worker's advocate in court presenting the case in an agreed manner.

3. *Legal Member of the Team.* As a team member the solicitor attends case conferences, case discussions etc., takes part in making the decision whether to take court proceedings, and collaborates with the social worker at all stages in the decision-making process.

To explore the interrelationships between manning, organisation and role definition, the situation for each of the local authorities studied is described. Subsequently the expectations social workers have of the role and the perception of the role relationships between social workers and solicitors are examined.

Authority 1

The legal department in this Authority is a part of the Town Clerks Department and is divided into two branches, one servicing local authority committees and the other doing pure legal work. The solicitor responsible for social services work is a senior assistant solicitor and has responsibilities in both branches of the department. He estimated his workload as 45% spent on social services legal work, (mostly child care cases), 20% spent on committee work (servicing social services committees) and 35% on other legal work, e.g. town planning. A senior assistant solicitor on the legal side also spent about 10% of his time on social services legal work. Apart from minimal clerical and secretarial help the solicitor has no real administrative or legal back-up. However, the solicitor said he was not really under pressure; holidays and sickness absences were dealt with by timetabling hearings.

The solicitor is closely linked into all social services work and does both their legal work and services the Social Services Committee. He is also chairman of the Area Review Committee and comes into regular contact with the Assistant Director of Social Services (fieldwork). In handling child care cases social workers often involve the solicitor directly in decisions, and he attends and chairs most case conferences. There are some instances where social workers take the initial decision themselves. The administrative tasks related to court hearings are shared between social worker, solicitor and courts officer

depending on their workloads. The tasks of case preparation (taking witness statements, preparing evidence, etc.) are done by the solicitor, with the assistance of the social worker. The solicitor visits area offices, has discussions with the social workers and studies the files. The solicitor in this Authority likes to do all the court advocacy and usually does not employ barristers, even in the high court.

The solicitor preferred to see his role as that of a 'team member'. He said social workers contacted him when they had cases with a legal angle where they felt action should be taken. He would then meet and discuss the case with them and would try to be more involved than purely as a legal advisor. Ideally he felt the social worker should decide on the short and long term management of a case and the solicitor's job was to help achieve these objectives by using the law.

Authority 2

The County Secretary's Department in this Authority is organised according to the main functional departments of the local authority (including social services) with the addition of a legal services department handling litigation. The solicitors responsible for taking child care cases to court are located in the legal services department. They have no direct links with the department which handles all committee and non-litigation work for the Social Services.

At the time of this study there were no formal contact or liaison arrangements between the solicitors handling cases with either the Social Services Department or Social Services Committee, although by the end of the period contacts were being established. The Social Services Department was viewed as one client department amongst others. The child care work load of the department is seen as the cream of the legal work and a very sensitive area, the work being done by experienced solicitors.

The decision to take a case to court is ultimately a social work decision with the solicitors taking a low-key role. The solicitors do not usually attend case conferences, and do not always meet with the social workers. Contact is frequently confined to telephone calls and letters. All the administrative work is done by the legal department, often by staff other than solicitors (legal executives). In the preparation of a case the solicitors expect the social workers to provide information and the legal department staff then take statements and prepare the case for court. The solicitors did not see rehearsal of witnesses, discussions of cases, or training social workers in court procedure, as part of their job. The solicitors did all the court advocacy in the juvenile court and preferred to do so in other courts wherever they had a right of audience. However in some of the cases in the study it was noted that they did brief counsel in response to pressure from the Social Services or their own department.

The solicitors saw themselves primarily as 'legal consultants': they expected (although accepted this did not happen) a well-prepared 'brief' from the social worker, on which they would give advice on the law, or complicating issues. They both thought that their primary function was the presentation of the case to the court and their overriding responsibility was as 'officers of the court'.

They felt that a solicitor needed to maintain his detachment from the case, in order to be able to cross-examine witnesses effectively. Both solicitors felt strongly this type of role model was best suited to local authority court work in general because of the overall responsibility to the authority and not the individual client.

In terms of operating the role as legal consultant both solicitors felt in man-power and time terms they were adequately equipped to deal with their work. They could use support staff to get proofs etc., and the two solicitors could attend all hearings. Distance between the area offices constrained pre-court meetings with social workers. The solicitors felt that most points could be adequately dealt with on the telephone, although they realised that social workers preferred meetings to telephone calls. However they felt that social workers always expected the solicitor to visit their office rather than vice versa. They viewed this attitude as unrealistic in view of the personnel available.

Authority 3

In this Authority the work of social services is done by two departments of the County Secretary's Department: personal services (management work, committee work, S.2 resolutions, etc.) and legal services (litigation). The solicitor responsible for child care cases is located in the legal services section and does exclusively court work. There is one designated solicitor for social services child care cases, spending 70/80% of time on this work. It is recognised throughout the department that this time is insufficient and the pressure of work is great. In practice the solicitor has no legal executive support. Despite obviously inadequate staffing, recruitment is prevented by a policy decision of the council to restrict the size of the establishment. The department has therefore had to devise an elaborate back-up system; firstly drawing on in-house solicitors and if necessary putting the work out to the private sector.

The County Secretary's Department liaises with the Social Services Depart-ment through a management committee on which all departments are represented at top management level. The solicitor responsible for child care cases has no formal contact or liaison with social services other than contacts with social workers on cases and indirectly through the Assistant County Secretary, (personal services) who is regarded as being an expert in the area and who sometimes acts in cases.

The decision to go to court is usually made by social workers in this authority. The solicitor is invited to case conferences, but can only attend occasionally. At case conferences the solicitor advises on the grounds to use and whether there is sufficient evidence in the case. The administrative tasks of obtaining dates and serving notices are usually done by the social workers although the solicitor may advise on time-tabling hearings and ensuring that witnesses are available. The solicitor usually asks the social worker to give a summary of the case on the telephone, to send copies of papers and tries to see the social worker at least once before the hearing. The social worker arranges for witnesses to be available. The solicitor spends more time with newer social workers explaining the shape of a case, court procedure, etc., to them, and regards this as part of the job of a local authority solicitor.

The solicitor would prefer to do both preparation and advocacy in all cases. However due to overload, cases were often farmed out to private practice. The solicitor recognised that using private solicitors relieved the pressure of work on the legal department and meant that social workers got more help than they would otherwise get. However the solicitor also mentioned that the use of external solicitors was expensive, did not relieve the department of all the work (e.g. monitoring), involved a degree of duplication, and that private solicitors did not have the same concentration of experience as a local authority solicitor. Wardship cases are usually handled by briefing counsel and counsel are briefed in appeals since the solicitor has no right of audience.

The solicitor would prefer the role of being a legal member of a team but in practice had little time to act as more than a legal consultant being informed initially about the case and asked about difficult legal points. In some cases the solicitor had more time to act as the social work advocate and would be more involved. The manpower constraints largely determined the role the solicitor could play. In addition this Authority is very large and some area offices are 40 miles away from county hall, further limiting the solicitor's ability to play an active role in cases.

Authority 4

The legal services department is unified, within the County Secretary's Department. The two solicitors responsible for child care cases are located within the department at assistant solicitor level. The senior solicitor spends 50/60% of his time on child care cases and the other approximately 80%. Towards the end of the study period the junior solicitor left and a newly qualified solicitor in the department was being given experience of child care cases. The head of department had had experience of child care cases and would provide occasional back-up. However there was an anticipated staff shortage after the departure of the junior solicitor who would not be replaced because of local authority cuts in expenditure. Some executive back-up was provided by a law clerk, amounting to a few hours per day, for sending out notices, etc.

There is no formal liaison between solicitors and Social Services but both solicitors are very interested in child care cases and know many of the social workers. The solicitors and social workers both take part in making decisions to go to court, the grounds and sufficiency of evidence. The solicitors both feel they should take part in decisions because they are employed by the local authority and represent the local authority in court. The administrative tasks of arranging court dates, notices, etc. are all done by the legal department. In preparing a case for court the social worker produces notes for the solicitor or fills in a form, and discusses it with the solicitor.

The solicitors in this Authority always do their own advocacy. They did not see Social Services as clients in the traditional sense. They saw themselves as taking part in the whole sequence working in conjunction as a 'team member' with the social worker. In court they saw themselves as representing the local authority. They explicitly mentioned the fact that they expected to influence decisions, and saw themselves as part of the decision-making team engaged in corporate decision-making.

During the study there were no factors which constrained the adoption of the 'team' model. However by the end of the period the legal department was planning to curtail the solicitor's activities because of manpower shortages. This was to be achieved by the solicitors being more selective in attending case conferences and the social workers being asked to provide more written information from the outset.

Authority 5

The legal department in this Authority is the successor to the Town Clerk's Department. One solicitor at assistant solicitor level is responsible for all social services work including servicing the Social Services Committee, servicing the Area Review Committee and all juvenile court work. The solicitor has the assistance of a clerk, and there are two back up solicitors who are able to cover court hearings during absences. The solicitor is responsible for liaison with the Social Services at grass-roots, management and committee levels.

The solicitor goes to all case conferences and discusses cases with social workers. The solicitor does all the administrative tasks: issuing notices, arranging of dates, etc. In the preparation of the case for court the solicitor always interviews witnesses personally, works in conjunction with the social worker and studies the files. The solicitor arranges for inexperienced witnesses (including social workers) to arrive early at court and goes through the evidence and procedures. The solicitor always does the advocacy in court. The only time counsel are briefed are for wardship cases which are contested.

The solicitor sees the role as being the social workers' advocate: the solicitor advising the social worker on a course of action but ultimately taking instructions, although would make an objection in writing to the area officer if there was a disagreement. In practice the solicitor follows the model of a legal member of team: taking part in all the discussions leading to a decision to take proceedings and working in conjunction with the social worker in deciding which witnesses to call and evidence to bring, etc. The solicitor had no constraints in terms of manpower or time on the role adopted. Distances did not affect the solicitor's ability to keep contacts with social workers or to attend events.

When appointed the solicitor was inexperienced in the law and advocacy in the juvenile court, although had had other advocacy experience. In learning the role the solicitor had help from the previous incumbent regarding the law, etc., and more general advice from the principal child care officer about case conferences and committee work. The solicitor was interested in and actively made efforts to obtain and maintain knowledge of social work practices and child care. Owing to complaints from social services regarding the previously high turnover of solicitors the head of legal department had undertaken always to provide an induction period for future solicitors.

The local authority legal departments and the roles played by the solicitors are each rather different in character. The main points are summarised in Table II.

Table II Main Organisational and Role Characteristics of Local Authority Legal Departments

	Authority				
	(1)	(2)	(3)	(4)	(5)
Number of Solicitors (child care)	1	2	1	2	1
Professional Manpower (in man equivalents)	0.55	1.10	.75	1.35	.60
Admin/ Clerical Support	Minimal Clerical	Good	Minimal	Some	Some
Involvement with Social Services Committees	Yes	No	No	No	Yes
Role Definition	Team Member	Legal Consultant	Legal Consultant/ Social Worker Advocate	Team Member	Social Worker Advocate/ Team Member
Any Constraints on Role/Task Performance	No	Physical Distance	Manpower Physical Distance	No	No

These characteristics will be referred to in the following sections covering social workers' views of the role of the solicitor and the relationships between the solicitors and social workers.

Social worker views of the role of the local authority solicitor

Social workers do not have clearly formed views of their expectations of the solicitor. Their views are often vague and internally inconsistent. This is not surprising since contact between individual social workers and the local authority solicitor is relatively rare in the normal course of work. The solicitor is often located at some distance from the area offices and contact during the preparation of a case may be mainly through letters and telephone calls. The role of the solicitor is not a topic which is normally discussed within area teams although the activities of the solicitor may be a subject for informal comment. In general there is no mutual examination of the role and role relationship between the area teams and the legal department. Such discussions may take place at senior management level but do not involve those staff responsible for day-to-day contact.

Most social workers expect that the solicitor will be involved in some way in the preparation of a case (67% spontaneously mentioned that they would contact him if they had a case where legal proceedings might be involved and 21% agreed when probed). Older social workers and those with more experience were more immediately aware of the need to consult the legal department. When the legal department is consulted about a case there is an expectation that the solicitor should be a 'child care' specialist and have a high level of expert knowledge on all aspects of child care law and the courts.

Social workers are less clear about the part the legal department should play in the decision phase of case preparation: 64% thought they would invite the solicitor to case conferences; a further 16% would do so when the social worker thought legal knowledge was needed or in relation to a difficult case. This was more common in Authority 5 (77%) and Authority 4 (74%) where the solicitors actively try to attend case conferences and less common in Authority 3 (37% said No) and when manpower limitations and distance may make the practice more difficult. Expectations about the role to be played by the solicitor at case conferences seem somewhat contradictory. Some social workers look to the solicitor for guidance and help in making a decision. Others think that if he does make suggestions or indicates strong reservations about the case he is interfering with the social workers' responsibility and professional judgement. On the one hand the social workers want the lawyer to give credence to social work concerns (and complain if he restricts himself to legal aspects). On the other, they resent his intrusion if he draws attention to social work elements in the decision, such as availability of proper placements.

Generally social workers expect that the solicitor or a substitute (in some cases a private solicitor) will present the case in court and considerable stress is placed on the need for 'good advocacy'. With comparatively little experience of courtroom technique, social workers tend to have very high expectations of their solicitors' standard of advocacy and seem to expect a forceful and well organised performance. They are most critical of solicitors who they perceive as vague, uncertain or anxious.

In summary, social workers tend to be ill-informed as to the kind of service they can expect from the solicitor in terms of time and volume of work. They are ambivalent about the extent to which the solicitor should influence decisions in relation to the case, but they do expect a high standard of knowledge and skills. In general discussions of the role of the solicitor social workers confirmed that they had not thought out what they expected from the solicitor and that sometimes their expectations were unreasonable. It should be said, however, that social workers are probably not dissimilar to solicitors' other clients in their expectations.

Role relationship between local authority solicitors and social workers

Social workers were asked for their general feelings about the local authority legal department:

    23% were very positive saying the department was very helpful, cooperative, etc.

27% were positive; the department was helpful, easy to work with, approachable, etc.

17% were neutral; they are OK; reasonable

19% were negative; the department is not easy to work with, difficult, terrible, appalling, etc.

18% did not know; had no experience.

The feelings about the legal department varied between the five authorities both in the distributions of opinion and in the specific comments that were made.

In Authority 1 there were many social workers who had been in post a comparatively short time and had had no contact with the solicitor and this was reflected in a high proportion who had no views (33%). Of those who did express a view nearly half expressed reservations, particularly about the solicitor's style of advocacy. While social workers appreciated the solicitor's concern and involvement in child care cases, they sometimes perceived this concern as intrusive and on occasions as interfering with the social worker's responsibility for the case. The preference for the team member role expressed by the solicitor in this authority, is not shared by many social workers. Their expectations were for the role to be that of 'social work advocate' with particular emphasis on the effective presentation of cases in court.

In Authority 2 a considerable degree of tension existed in the relationships between the social service area offices and the legal department. Half the social workers interviewed expressed negative attitudes to the department. Specific comments centred on a perceived lack of expertise of the solicitor; he was thought not to be a specialist in child care law, not to possess sufficient knowledge, not to be competent and efficient and this was thought to be evident in inadequate preparation of the cases. The solicitor in this authority is responsible for doing work for other departments in the authority although, as a department, Social Services takes the largest percentage of his time. The relationships with other departments appear to be much more straightforward. The departmental staff collect and prepare the information for the case and the solicitor acts as a barrister would in private practice giving an opinion on the case and presenting it in court. The solicitor in question probably does not conceal his preference for this more clear-cut relationship and social workers believe he prefers other kinds of work and is not sympathetic to social work concerns. There seems to be no reason to doubt both the competence and knowledge of the solicitor concerned; he was one of the only two local authority solicitors directly handling child care cases in the study who had had prior experience of these cases in other authorities and several of the private solicitors interviewed in the area spoke highly of his expertise.

As in Authority 1, social workers' expectations of the role were at variance with the view expressed by solicitors. They thought that the solicitor should be more prepared to discuss the cases with social workers and be more personally involved. In general they were unaware of the limited amount of time available for case preparation and travelling to area offices for meetings. There was also clashes of personal styles with social workers seeing the solicitors as legalistic, formal and remote.

It was clear during fieldwork and it is also reflected in the distribution of attitudes, that there had been a degree of polarisation between the legal department and the area offices. Social workers' attitudes seemed often to be reflecting group rather than individual views. It was observed throughout the study that area offices, and teams within those offices, formed coherent social groups around which accounts of recent experiences were very rapidly passed, not always accurately. A particularly outstanding incident could achieve the status of a local myth which was retailed to the research team, with variations, by members of the staff. Few social workers had sufficient first hand contact with the legal department to test the reality of these stories and there appeared to be no mechanisms by which they could be examined and any problems sorted out.

Once a group view gains currency, new situations will be approached in the light of existing expectations. For example, in the preparation of cases once there is a belief that things do go wrong then events will be approached within that framework: minor misunderstandings will be seen as major disagreements; messages will be perceived as carrying covert information quite other than their overt content, and in extreme cases information will simply not be conveyed. This kind of phenomenon is not uncommon in relationships between departments in many kinds of organisation. It can still have seriously debilitating effects and needs to be recognised and dealt with. By the end of the study the legal department and the social services department were making joint efforts to improve relationships and to achieve mutual understanding.

The difficulties encountered in relationships between the legal department and social workers in authority 2 are by no means unique. Elements of the problem were also present in other authorities included in the study and discussions with other research workers and practitioners suggest that other authorities have had similar experiences.

In Authority 3 geographical distances and inadequate staffing have meant that there has been little contact between many of the social workers and the solicitor. About one third of social workers said they had no views on the legal department for these reasons. Another 20% had reservations about the service from the department and in particular commented on what they saw as the solicitor's lack of advocacy skills. However they spoke well of the level of expert knowledge and help they could draw on.

In this authority a strong preference was expressed for using private solicitors to present the local authority case. This preference is partly historical since the practice of using private solicitors used to be widespread in the authority and is still comparatively common. But the preference also reflects the social workers' wish to develop a personal relationship with a local solicitor over time and the convenience of physical proximity. There was also a belief that local, private solicitors offered better advocacy skills than were normally available from the legal department of the authority. The use of private solicitors to represent the local authority is likely to continue because of current restrictions on recruiting staff despite the recognition that this is a more expensive alternative.

In Authority 4, 90% of social workers viewed the service they received from the legal department positively and none gave negative answers. Specific

comments emphasised the thoroughness of case preparation and the competence and efficiency of the two solicitors involved. The efforts made by the solicitors to become part of the decision-making team was reflected in comments by social workers that the members of the legal department were concerned and interested in social work. The only problem reported in this authority by some social workers was that they found it difficult to contact the solicitor involved in a case. Since the solicitors spend a considerable amount of time in court and out of the office, some difficulties in making contact are inevitable.

In considering the success of the current relationship with the legal department in this authority it seemed to us that the solicitors had carefully considered the role that it was appropriate for them to play in care proceedings. They had concluded that they should be much more actively involved in case management than would normally be characteristic of solicitors in private practice, and that they should 'sell' their services to their clients. They had also the personal skills to put these conclusions into operation. They were also fortunate that neither manpower constraints nor excessive travelling requirements had restricted their role performance to that time.

In Authority 5 the social worker views of the legal department were also predominantly positive (66% positive comments and no negative). Specific comments reflected the extent of the case preparation and the efforts made by the solicitor to work with the social workers in preparing the case, as well as a fluent and competent style of advocacy (e.g. prepare case well, thorough, efficient, competent, good advocate). Social workers mentioned that the solicitor always has time and is easy to contact reflecting the fact that this solicitor does nothing but social services work, is working in a geographically compact area, has a relatively small number of cases per year and consequently has more time available for each case. There had been unsatisfactory relationships with the legal department in the past and considerable and conscious efforts were being made to improve the situation.

The patterns of attitudes described above for each authority emphasise the differences in the way roles are performed and in the interrelationships which exist. There are bound to be many other variations which could be observed in other authorities. In the following discussion we shall consider three issues which arose in one way or another in all 5 authorities and which are in our judgement, central to understanding and improving the relationships between social workers and local authority solicitors where the need for improvement exists.

1. Expectations

From both interview material and from observation and discussion it is clear that social workers have very high expectations of the standard of service they should get from local authority solicitors. They expect the solicitor to be highly competent in a range of skills which do not necessarily reside in the same person viz: formal legal knowledge, knowledge of social work and local practice, advocacy, organisational and administrative skills. They expect the solicitor to have time to spend on the case, to be available when required and to be sympathetic and concerned.

In considering the reasons for these rather unrealistic expectations it must first be noted that social workers are often unaware of the organisational, workload and manpower constraints governing the legal department. They do not know what it is reasonable to expect and do not realise that their expectations are unrealistic. However, it is not only a matter of lack of information. Social workers look to their solicitor to inject confidence and certainty into cases where risky decisions may need to be made and those decisions are subject to scrutiny by the courts. If a solicitor does manage to communicate a sense of confidence and is able to reduce anxiety he will be highly regarded. When a solicitor increases anxiety, whether by lack of confidence in himself, aloofness or apparent muddle, the negative feelings aroused are very strong. This may be more to do with the projection of anxiety about care cases which should be dealt with in other ways, than a true reflection of the nature and styles of solicitors. However it may also be the case that the selection processes for solicitors to work on social service cases do not reflect the skill mix which the job requires.

Information sharing and discussions would probably go a long way to achieving shared expectations and understanding between social workers and members of the legal department. Discussions at management level about the standard of service needed and provided by the legal department, and about policy priorities could also be helpful in those authorities where this is not already done. If there are unresolved anxieties about care proceedings these should be made explicit and ways found of giving support to social workers, rather than allowing them to distort the relationship with the solicitor.

2. Role and Task Agreements

In the relationships between the legal department and social work area offices there is in general an absence of formal agreements and procedures on the role relationships between the departments and the allocation of tasks in care proceedings. Some work may have been done by one side alone, or in relation to particular topics, such as the handling of 'education' cases. But the general impression is that the relationship has not received explicit and joint attention. Even in Authority 4 where the solicitors have developed a well thought out approach to the role, this is not shared with the social workers. When the relationship is going well there seems little reason to make formal agreements about tasks and roles since the good relationships will allow informal methods to make up any deficiency in the system. When goodwill does not exist or the relationship has become distorted then the lack of agreements may become more serious.

Arising from an analysis of the relationship in task and responsibility terms and the observation of particular instances of miscommunication we can sugggest three areas which could benefit from closer and joint examination by the two departments.

(a) *Location of responsibility and authority.* Because of the management and supervision structure of a social work team, decisions are usually taken after discussion between several social workers. Who carries responsibility for the decision and who implements various aspects of the decision taken may not be

made explicit. In a difficult case the social worker, his team leader and the area director may all be involved and take some part in decisions and events relating to the preparation of the case for court. This may be clear and acceptable to the social workers but it can be confusing for the solicitor. This is particularly so if on the social work side there is not total agreement and shared information. The solicitor is accustomed to having 'a client' who has authority to give him instructions. In the normal way he would probably act as if the social worker was his client. But if people with management roles contact him about the case, who then should he see as the client? Where does he obtain his authority to prepare the case in a particular way? If he seeks guidance from the wrong person he can create ill-will amongst the social work staff.

(b) *Tasks in case preparation.* The decisions about which witnesses to call are crucial to the preparation of a case. While it is desirable to have witnesses who can give first hand evidence on all the facts relating to proving the case, this must be balanced against practical considerations of the difficulty of getting a large number of people to court on a given date, interviewing them and checking their evidence and not taking up too much court time with unnecessary witnesses. The solicitor may regard these decisions as within his expertise. The social worker, however, is in possession of the information relating to the case and he may feel he is in the best position to know who should be called. During the phase of case preparation, responsibility for the management of the case may shift from the social worker to the solicitor and it is desirable that there is mutual agreement about these shifts and where responsibilities lie at each stage. As can be seen from the description of the 5 authorities these decisions are handled in different ways and it is preferable that everyone is clear as to the system they are operating.

(c) *Handling complaints.* The third area in which there is a case for the development of more formal mechanisms or agreements for handling the relationship between social workers and the legal department is what could loosely be called a 'grievance machinery'. No system is ever perfect and from time to time misunderstandings and inefficiencies will occur. A well designed system should include an agreed way of handling any such difficulties. If a social worker thinks the solicitor has handled a case badly or the solicitor thinks the social worker has performed badly as a witness, there should be means of raising the matter. Without such a mechanism neither side has the opportunity to obtain feedback which may help with their own learning or to put their side of the case in their own defence. If such issues are not resolved they may become 'legendary' and sour future relationships not only between the individuals concerned but also between the whole social services team or office and the legal department. At present the organisational level at which the two departments formally connect is usually at a senior departmental level. Where this is used to handle comparatively trivial complaints the conflict can be escalated and the possibility of finding amicable solutions decreased.

These aspects of the role relationships between the legal department and social workers are comparatively trivial. They cause little or no difficulty where there is sympathy between the personalities involved or where the solicitor makes a special effort. However no large scale bureaucracy can guarantee

always to get the right person in the job or for him to have the time or the inclination to make special efforts. The fact that informal relationships make up for the deficiencies of the formal system in some cases is no argument for allowing deficiencies in the system to remain.

3. Staff Turnover and Lack of Continuity in Relationships

As mentioned above, the current organisation of legal departments and career structure for local authority lawyers creates a situation where solicitors handling child care cases are relatively young, likely to be inexperienced in this field of law and to only stay in the job for about 3 years. Social services people feel that they are just starting to get good services from a particular solicitor when he leaves. Even if there were not organisational constraints and lack of promotion prospects for a lawyer specialising in this field there are probably only a few solicitors who would wish to continue doing social service work for more than a few years. From a lawyer's point of view this area of law is a highly specialised and narrow one and in purely legal terms not particularly complicated or stretching.

Social workers and social services management emphasise the need for continuity. Social workers would like to be able to build up a personal relationship with their legal representatives based on face-to-face contact. Since the contact over particular cases is relatively infrequent this process normally takes a number of years. In addition to the wish for personalised contact there is also an underlying feeling that lawyers coming into social services work need to undergo a socialisation process. Solicitors may need to learn about matter which are not primarily legal; the nature, organisation and language of social work, the local system of agencies and personnel, the local courts and magistrates. The complexity and individuality of these localised and informal systems certainly do require a learning period to be operated successfully. However there is another level at which it is implied that solicitors need to be encouraged to abandon their purely legal views of cases and to adopt a wider, welfare view. In particular this attitude emerges in relation to the standards of evidence required to prove social services cases. It has been reported that solicitors first coming to child care cases frequently take the view that, on the evidence available, the cases should not be taken to court. Whether it is by learning that there is a wider range of material which contribute to the decision to take care proceedings than can ever be produced as formal evidence or by an acceptance of the standards of proof being operated by the courts, most solicitors have usually abandoned their initial views after a few years in the job.

It must of course be pointed out that there is a fairly high rate of turnover in social work staff as well as amongst solicitors. However since social workers are part of a team and an office, continuity of relationships can be preserved, particularly by senior members of staff. Personalised relationships can be handed on from one social worker to another. When problems are encountered, the difficulty can be handled by a long-standing member of the team who does have a personal relationship developed over time. When a solicitor leaves there is a much greater loss in continuity in the

interdepartmental relationships than when an individual social worker leaves.

Some of the difficulties in handling continuity could perhaps be lessened if legal departments adopted a more active induction and handover policy for new recruits such as has been developed in Authority 5. Where there are two solicitors engaged in child care cases a new recruit can be introduced gradually. A round of visits to area offices to introduce the new man would also bear dividends. However it is probably the case that if issues of role expectations and the role responsibilities between the two departments were given greater attention the need for continuity of personnel would diminish.

Private solicitors

Private solicitors normally become involved in care proceedings as the representative of the child when it is the child who is party to the proceedings and entitled to legal aid. Solicitors may also on occasions represent parents.

Solicitors' practices vary a good deal in size and staffing from, for example, a two- or three-man practice using a single office (15 in the sample) to a large practice with many offices and a departmental structure for different types of business (12 solicitors worked in practices with 4 or more offices). If a practice deals with children's cases there are usually one or two solicitors who take the work either in the context of matrimonial cases or contentious business (litigation, court work, etc.). In towns or cities with one magistrates court a small number of practices handle child care cases and individuals gain a reputation in the area with cases referred to them by courts, social services, CABs, etc. In large cities and particularly London the number and range of solicitors' practices leads to a much more diffuse pattern with expertise concentrated in specialist practices and law centres.

A solicitor accepting a brief to represent a child in care proceedings is confronted with a number of practical and ethical difficulties. There is a good deal of uncertainty and disagreement about how the role of the representative of a child should be defined and what might constitute effective role performance. Solicitors often receive no training in handling the complex role issues which may arise in what could loosely be called 'welfare law'. There is also very little written in what, in terms of the whole of legal practice, is a very specialist area. Occasionally there is some discussion of the problems of representing a child (e.g. Hayes, 1978) or a specification of the tasks which a representation of the child should undertake (Feldman, 1976).

The majority of solicitors made it clear that they saw the role as a difficult one, some being extremely outspoken about the anomalies both in the law and in court practice. Only nine did not appear to perceive the role as problematic. Most solicitors were able to articulate an approach to the role, even if only in terms of the tasks they would expect to perform (only nine were unable to do so). However the approaches to the role varied widely.

In content analysing descriptions of the role of representative of the child given by solicitors we found that their responses could be divided into two main types: those which described the role principally in terms of the presentation of information and those which were concerned with the decisional elements involved in the interpretation of information. Within each type

individual solicitors took up different stances. In the following sections the role of the solicitor is discussed under these main headings. In each case the responses given by solicitors are preceded by a more general discussion of the nature of the role and tasks involved.

1. Information Presentation

Information presentation is always important in the role of a solicitor whether he briefs counsel or appears in court himself. However this element in his role is most apparent when he acts as advocate. As part of his duty to the court the advocate must seek to put before the court all matters relevant to its decision. This responsibility exists even if the material may be prejudicial to his client. In adversarial proceedings where the contesting parties are represented, the presentation of disadvantageous information can usually be left to the advocate on the other side, particularly to the prosecution in criminal cases. (Although as DuCann (1980) points out, this can still be a problem in criminal cases.) However, in care proceedings, particularly those in which the parents are not represented, this responsibility of the advocate may create difficulty. For example, the solicitor representing the child may be convinced of the need to remove a child from its parents to protect it from physical harm and is not opposing the local authority case. He may however be in possession of information which could be damaging to the local authority's case. The parents are not represented and cannot raise the matter, should he introduce the prejudicial material? The professional solution to this dilemma is to introduce the material since the law requires the applicant, i.e. the local authority, to prove its case and for the court to decide on its merits. Also, since the solicitor is likely to appear in that court again it is in his interests to preserve his reputation as a disinterested and trustworthy professional.

The advocate must seek to put before the court the relevant information in a clear, orderly, and intelligible way. First he does this by calling and examining witnesses. Witnesses with relevant, first hand experience must be found and assisted in presenting their information by being asked guiding but not leading questions. Second he may cross examine witnesses called by other parties. He may seek to elicit or clarify information. Or he may test evidence already given. By cross-checking or by challenging statements he may seek to provide the court with information about the likely reliability and validity of the statements made. Third, he may address the court summarising and reviewing the information relevant to the decision, emphasising some points and not others.

In carrying out these tasks the advocate uses his verbal fluency, his ability to order and structure information and his ability to identify ambiguities and gaps in information as it is presented to the court. He also draws on his knowledge of the court and the law. Information is selected and presented according to its relevance within the rules of evidence and in the language in which the court works. In representing his client the solicitor places these skills at the disposal of his client. This is clearly of benefit to clients without verbal skills, as is the case of a young child, the relatively uneducated, or the frightened and may also be an advantage to the articulate who are unfamiliar with the courts' frame of reference.

In the majority of cases, solicitors representing the child do their own advocacy in the juvenile court. In our sample 32 solicitors said that they always do their own advocacy, 6 said sometimes and 12 said they do not. At the time of the study there was no provision for briefing counsel on the legal aid scheme. A solicitor could decide to pay counsel out of his own fees and some practices did this as being a cheaper alternative to the solicitor attending court. This was more common in London where there is a large pool of inexperienced and 'cheap' barristers. In some practices care cases are handled by legal executives or clerks who have no right of audience in the magistrates court and therefore cannot do their own advocacy. Both of these factors operate in relation to London practices; in the London borough 9/10 solicitors never did their own advocacy whereas in all the other areas only 3/40 never did.

The information presentation aspect of the role of the solicitor representing the child can be pursued more or less actively. From the answers given by the solicitors we interviewed three different stances emerged.

(a) A relatively *passive stance* in which the solicitor confines himself to clarifying information presented by other parties. He does not call any witnesses himself and restricts his cross examination to filling in obvious gaps or going over ground which did not appear to have been clear. He tends not to impose any clear structure on the information. This may be called the 'watchdog' role. Five solicitors in the sample described their role exclusively in these terms.

(b) *'Testing the evidence':* the solicitor does not introduce his own witnesses but pursues a more active cross examination of the other parties' witnesses aimed at making sure the case has been proved. Ten solicitors saw their role in this way.

(c) A more *active stance* in which the solicitor takes part in the production of new information to the court either by calling his own witnesses or questioning witnesses about matters not previously raised of which he thinks the court should be aware. Five solicitors described their role in these terms.

Thus overall, 20 of the 50 solicitors interviewed described their role in terms of the presentation of information. These three positions represent the way in which solicitors discuss the role of the representative of the child. They are also clearly recognisable in the behaviour of solicitors in court and this will be discussed in relation to the cases we observed. Whether in practice a solicitor carries out his conception of the role may vary according to the circumstances of the particular case.

2. The Interpretation of Information to Form a Case

The advocate may go further than simply presenting information: he may present to the court a particular view of the matter, argue for an interpretation of events or seek a given outcome. To do so involves the advocate in decisions about the interpretation of events and judgements about what to do in the best interests of his client. When any professional makes such judgements he draws

on his professional knowledge and experience. He is ethically bound not to abuse his position of authority by imposing judgements on his client which arise from his personal attitudes and emotions. In the area of child care law the solicitor depends more on his personal experience than on a codified body of knowledge. It is also an area which arouses strong feelings. In these circumstances there is a greater risk that judgements will be made on personal rather than professional criteria, although the professional may be unaware that this is so.

Solicitors traditionally handle the decisional issues by 'taking instructions'. For example, in criminal cases decisions as to plea and interpretation of events are seen as coming from the client in the form of instructions. The solicitor may offer advice on the likely consequences of the client's decisions in the light of his knowledge of the courts and the law. The client may wish to modify his decisions accordingly. However even in the criminal law this is undoubtedly an oversimplification and the solicitor is much more active in the decisional process than is normally admitted. Clients may be looking for guidance from their solicitor; they may interpret his advice as being more directive than was intended; solicitors may be more directive than they themselves realise. Lawyers are extremely sensitive to any suggestion that they force their clients to accept interpretations of their case as any discussion of plea bargaining demonstrates (Baldwin and McConville, 1977). It is the court which is sanctioned to make decisions about the merits of a case. Solicitors must not pre-empt that decision and thus act as a barrier preventing their client gaining access to the court's decision. It should be noted that a solicitor may refuse to represent a client if he has strong feelings on the matter and a client may take his case to another solicitor if he is dissatisfied with the advice he receives.

The representative of a child is in a peculiarly difficult position when it comes to taking instructions. A young child clearly cannot give instructions and there are difficulties about whether an older child can take decisions about what is in his own interests. Some solicitors take the position that if the client cannot give him instructions then he cannot adopt any stance in court and must reject this aspect of the role altogether. Out of the 41 solicitors who could articulate the role 20 did not conceive of it in interpretation terms. 13 made explicit reference to the fact that it is up to the court to decide, e.g.

'There is almost no role at all. You can't take sides because that would be making a decision yourself and pre-empting the magistrate's decision.'

'I don't like acting for the child. I feel as though I am being placed in the position of having to make a judgement and I am not qualified to do so.'

'You have to put yourself in the position of trying to do your best for the child. I don't like doing that because it is the court's function.'

In the case of older children 18 solicitors say that they take instructions in the same way as from an adult; 27 said that they would consider other things, although they would put the child's views to the court as relevant information.

The solicitor representing the child may be prepared to argue that on the basis of the evidence of the applicant and his own investigations he should make up his own mind as to the stance he should take in court. This may involve accepting the views of other people, in particular the parent or the

social worker, and arguing from a stance based on their views. There are two related rationales which can be invoked in defence of this position:

(a) the adversarial method whereby different parties argue different cases, assists in the process of bringing out relevant information and reduces the risk of collusive suppression of information.

(b) in order to assist the court in making its decision it is helpful if the alternatives which must be decided between are clearly identified and the evidence presented in relation to each.

If the solicitor presents a view which is different from that of the applicant either of these rationales may apply. They do not however apply if the solicitor decides that the view of the applicant is the correct one and therefore does not oppose the case. If a solicitor does act in this way it can be argued that he has pre-empted the decision of the court. In the sample of solicitors interviewed 16 saw the role as involving the solicitor in investigating the case and making up his own mind.

The two groups of people who are likely to have views on the matter which could be taken up by the solicitor are the social workers and the parents. After considering the available evidence the solicitor may come to agree with either of these parties or he may see either of them as the source of his instructions.

The social worker is likely to possess the relevant information in relation to the case and to have evaluated the situation as it affects the child. Either out of regard for the expertise of the social worker or because of her informational advantage, the solicitor may well come to the same conclusion as to the best interests of the child. In addition the social worker or the social services may have obtained representation for the child and provided the solicitor with the case. (In the sample 29 solicitors said that they obtained most or some of their cases in this way; 13 said most.) However only one solicitor saw himself as being instructed by the social worker. He argued that in most cases the child is in the care of the local authority under a place of safety order or an interim care order and they are therefore *in loco parentis* for the child.

On the other hand the parents may have strong views both on the interpretation of events and on the disposal. As they are not party to the proceedings and are rarely represented their views may not be made clear or persuasively argued. Most solicitors believe that the parents should be represented and some are prepared to put this belief into practice despite the fact that the legal aid certificate is made out in the name of the child. Two solicitors argued that the local authority effectively acts in the interests of the child and the representation of the child can be left to them leaving the solicitor free to represent the parents. Another solicitor expressed the view that where the parents disagree with the local authority then this constitutes an alternative case which can be put before the court in order for the local authority case to be properly tested.

Solicitors may come to represent the child through an approach made to them by the parents: 14 said they receive most cases and 16 receive some cases from the parents. When cases come to a solicitor in this way he is usually faced with the difficult task of explaining that it is the child who is the one to be represented. Perhaps he is more likely to be influenced by the views of the

parents when he is approached by them. When representing the child 10 solicitors said that they would represent the views of the parents, particularly if they had made the approach to him. 22 said they would take the parents' views into account as part of the total picture. Although solicitors are likely to be influenced by the parents, and social workers widely believe them to be exclusively influenced by them, only one mentioned that whether he liked it or not he would be affected by hearing their side of the matter first.

The most difficult situation which confronts a solicitor who is inclined to the views of the parents are those cases where there is a clear conflict of interest between the parents and the child, especially in non-accidental injury cases. 5 solicitors specified that in these cases they would tell the parents to obtain separate representation for the child.

The principal difficulty confronting the solicitor who tries to make his own evaluation of the evidence is that he will need to deal with matters which are beyond his professional training. A number of solicitors commented on this, for example: 'I have to make a judgement and I am not qualified to do so. I know very little about child care, I don't like children and I don't have any. It's a terrible position to be in'. Several specifically commented that they are not expert in talking to children and would not therefore see the child. Others, particularly those with children themselves, felt that they would be as competent as anyone else to make an assessment of the situation of the child and the family. There is some merit in this view since in general the magistrates sitting on the juvenile bench have no greater expertise in the area than do the solicitors appearing before them.

In making assessments without the appropriate conceptual tools or knowledge in an area in which everyone has strongly entrenched attitudes and feelings the solicitor is vulnerable to being overinfluenced by his own feelings without being aware of it. He may also not see the significance of certain kinds of behaviour which professional training might suggest to be of considerable importance. In addition the local authority's case depends on the professional assessments of social workers and others. The solicitor for the child is unlikely to be equipped to make an appreciation of the strengths and weaknesses of these professional assessments. This inequality can give rise to the solicitor having a greater regard for the professional view and not challenging it sufficiently or a generalised hostility to what is seen as professional jargon and woolly thinking.

In view of the difficulties for the solicitor acting for the child either making up his own mind or taking up the views of the parents or the social worker, a few solicitors feel the need for an independent social work assessment. This may be either in the form of the guardian ad litem system envisaged by the 1975 Children Act or as an independent social work report commissioned by the solicitor. The fact that so few solicitors mention this solution to their obvious difficulties is perhaps not surprising since the 1975 act has not been implemented in any circumstances other than unopposed revocation proceedings and there is no generally available way for solicitors to obtain independent social work reports.

Without being able to draw upon professional advice, is there any way in which a solicitor representing the child can take up a stance on a case without

exceeding his professional expertise or distorting the intentions of the law by representing the parents?

In some cases the representative can clearly confine his decision-making to areas which lie within his professional expertise. At least in proceedings in the juvenile court the law sets out the grounds which must be proved for a case to succeed. On the basis of the evidence presented by the applicant the lawyer may be of the opinion that the evidence is insufficient or bears some other interpretation than that which is being argued by the applicant. He may then put that argument to the court for its consideration and question witnesses accordingly. While any advocate may adopt this stance in the appropriate circumstances, it is not one which can be readily applied in most care proceedings. It is also difficult in practice since the advocate may be unaware of the extent of the applicant's case until it has been presented in court.

Another possible position is to adopt what could be called 'technical opposition'. This involves arguing that to make a care order on a child and remove it from its parents is a very grave step and should be opposed. The local authority must prove that it has grounds within the terms defined by law, that other alternative ways of handling the case would not be adequate to meet the child's needs and that a care order is necessary to protect the child's interests. A solicitor adopting this stance will develop a coherent and systematic approach to the evidence and made extensive pre-hearing investigations. Three solicitors described their role in representing the child in these terms.

Despite the difficulties of a solicitor for the child adopting a stance in relation to a case there are some advantages in him doing so. There is likely to be a greater coherence and point to his questioning of witnesses and his submissions to the court. He is also likely to take a greater part in the proceedings and there will probably be a more thorough testing of the evidence and a greater chance that justice will seen to have been done.

3. Support Function

The role of the representative of the child has another dimension, namely that of support for the child; interpreting the court and its procedures to him. This is obviously more relevant in the case of an older child. Perhaps because the difficulties of representation tend to be concentrated around the young child none of the solicitors interviewed raised this aspect of their role. It is mentioned here since social workers often see this function as the main reason for the child being represented (see below).

Solicitors see the role of the representative of the child as a particularly difficult one and made more so when the parents are not separately represented. There are a wide range of solutions suggested to the role problems involved and the most commonly given are:

(a)   testing the evidence as it is presented in court (10);

(b)   investigating the case and making up my own mind as to an appropriate stance to take (16);

(c)   representing the parents (10).

There are difficulties associated with all these stances; in the case of (a) the solicitor may not make any real contribution to the proceedings; in (b) he may exceed his professional expertise and pre-empt the role of the court; and in (c) he may misuse the legal aid system and by-pass the intentions of the law.

Role of the representative of the parents. In the sample of solicitors interviewed, 39 had represented the parents in care proceedings at some time. Since the parent is not a party to the proceedings local juvenile courts tend to have developed different practices as to the part the parent may have to play in hearings. Under Rule 14 b) of the Magistrates Court Rules the parent is allowed to rebut any allegations made against him. Some courts will allow the parents to cross-examine witnesses, some to introduce their own witnesses and yet others treat the parent as full party to the proceedings. Only in relation to one juvenile court did any of the solicitors report restrictions on the part played by the parents in court. The main restriction on the representation of parents was seen to be the lack of legal aid.

The role of the representative of the parents is seen as a more straightforward one than that of representative of the child. Half the solicitors said that they saw their role as taking instructions from the parents rather than being concerned with the interests of the child. However a number felt that they should still consider the best interests of the child; 10 saw the child's interests as paramount. Where the solicitor comes to the conclusion that the child's interests are not best served by the wishes of the parent he would normally make this clear to the parent, leaving the parent with the option of obtaining alternative representation; 12 solicitors said that this is consistent with the way solicitors would behave in other areas of the law. However this practice is likely to act as an effective barrier to the parent obtaining representation. Only the most persistent parent is likely to take his case elsewhere and unless he does so the solicitor has effectively deprived him of representation.

The practicalities of representation. Whether the solicitor is representing the child or the parents the tasks he will perform and the difficulties he will encounter do not differ greatly. The main task elements of the solicitor acting in care proceedings can be described as follows:

1. Interview whoever engages him to establish the bones of the case, arrange for legal aid, etc,

2. Obtain information from the local authority on the grounds and the evidence on which they are bringing the case. This usually involves a telephone call to the social worker or local authority solicitor.

3. Interview parents, interview or see child, obtain statements and establish the points of disagreement with the local authority.

4. Consider and obtain further evidence, other witnesses, independent reports.

5. Obtain documentary evidence from the local authority; try to obtain or find out about the social enquiry report.

6. Consider the law and prepare the case for court.

Virtually all the solicitors said that they would interview the parents (46) and talk to the social worker (44); 17 would talk to the local authority solicitor. According to the nature of the case and the kind of co-operation received from the social worker the solicitor may have further interviews with the social worker, discuss points of disagreement and try to negotiate a compromise solution. Of other people who might be contacted for information or to act as witnesses, health visitors, General Practitioners, and other medical personnel are most frequently mentioned (17). Residential staff, foster parents, teachers, Education Welfare Officers and police are sometimes specified as people who might be contacted in appropriate cases. Ten solicitors mentioned that they would consider obtaining independent reports from experts; doctors, psychologists, psychiatrists or social workers. Ten said that they would visit the child's home or current placement. These two latter courses of action seem to distinguish the most thorough and careful approach to the preparation of a case.

The approaches to the preparation of the case can be categorised as follows:

(a) Minimal: obtaining information from the social worker and parent only (14 solicitors answered in this way);

(b) Standard: obtaining information from the parent, child, social worker and any relevant others (21 solicitors answered in this way);

(c) Maximum: the standard activities plus either obtaining independent reports or visiting the child's placement. (15 solicitors answered in this way).

It might be expected that those solicitors who see the role of the representative of the child as investigating the case and making up his own mind would see the need to make more extensive pre-hearing investigations than those adopting more formal or limited role definitions. In fact this is not the case. This finding makes it clear that at least some of the solicitors who are prepared to make a judgement about the right course of action in a case do so without realising the difficulties inherent in the role they have taken on. Those who see the role in terms of representing the parent tend to see only minimal preparation as appropriate.

For a solicitor to make all the investigations necessary for the preparation of a case for court can involve a considerable amount of time. About half the solicitors mentioned this aspect as a problem which could constrain their ability to prepare a case properly. If a place of safety order is taken on a child the solicitor may be notified quickly and thus have 28 days before the case comes to court. He may not however be contacted, particularly if the approach is made by the parents, until only a short time before the hearing. A few solicitors said that they were not prepared to have their preparation curtailed by time constraints and would always ask for an adjournment of the hearing if the time was not adequate. The time pressure may not be dealt with by adjourning the case since the pressure may derive more from the pressure of other work being handled by the solicitor at any one time. (10 said that this was a problem.) The pressure of work argument applies particularly to those solicitors who are mainly employed on legal aid cases where a high turnover of

cases is necessary if the work is to be economically viable.

Solicitors may also experience considerable difficulty in obtaining the information they require. The following problems were mentioned. Sixteen said that they had difficulty in obtaining information from the local authority. They mentioned un-cooperative social workers, difficulty in contacting the social worker and difficulties in obtaining documents as the main problems. Nineteen said that they had difficulty in obtaining information from parents. They said that parents can be unco-operative, hostile to the solicitor, aggressive and secretive. They may be inarticulate (7), of limited intelligence (8) or have problems speaking English. There may also be difficulties if the parents are separately represented (2). And of course it is difficult to obtain information from a young child. Finding witnesses who have first-hand information and who are prepared to give evidence in court can also be problematic (2). This applies to expert witnesses as well as ordinary witnesses. In addition there is uncertainty about whether the legal aid authorities will allow the cost of expert reports. (This was mentioned by 12 solicitors). Even if the solicitor sets out to make a thorough investigation of the case the practical difficulties of doing so may conspire to leave him unprepared to effectively represent the child at the court hearing.

Social workers' perceptions of the role of solicitors

Most of the social workers who were interviewed had been involved in a case in which a solicitor had represented their client (92%). But this by no means happens in all cases. (Always 6%; usually 27%; sometimes 25% and rarely 16%). For most social workers their contact with private solicitors is sporadic. The exceptions are team leaders of teams with a large child care case load or courts officers who over time may come to know individual solicitors quite well.

In general social workers believe that it is of benefit for a child to be represented in court proceedings. (69% said always of benefit; 24% sometimes, and 5% said no benefit.) A third of the social workers interviewed said that they would advise their clients to be represented in all circumstances. Others specified that they would advise representation in particular kinds of cases; in care proceedings (29%); when the client was opposed to the local authority's action (19%); when the client was pleading not guilty to a criminal charge (31%); when charged with a serious offence or when a custodial disposal order might be made (22%). Only very few said that they would ever discourage a client from being represented. The only circumstances in which this might arise was when the client could not afford the fees or when the charge involved was trivial. Social workers, like solicitors, are in favour of the parents being represented; 38% always, 27% sometimes but a substantial proportion did not know. However comparatively few mentioned the representation of parents as an improvement they would like to see in the system(12) and 24 said they thought parents should get legal aid.

Despite general support of the notion that representation is beneficial to the client, at least in some circumstances, social workers are often puzzled or

vague about the nature of the benefits or the role of the representative. The most common view of the role of the representative was that of a presenter of information (53%), and the benefit to the client as having his views presented articulately in court. Some saw the information presentation role in terms of 'testing the evidence' and bringing out all the facts (13%). In general social workers have little understanding or sympathy with the role of a solicitor in making a case on behalf of the child, particularly when that case conflicts with their own view. While 16% saw that it could be an advantage to the client to obtain an independent view of the case from the solicitor, it is more common for a solicitor's efforts in arguing a case to be seen as partisan, biased and concerned only with winning irrespective of the best interests of the child. Since social workers see themselves as acting in the best interests of the child it is not perhaps surprising that they see someone arguing for another view in this way. Although 29% saw the role of the solicitor as defending the legal interests of the client, 31% think that solicitors are too restricted in their views being only concerned with the legal aspects of the client's case.

Given social workers' own concerns with giving support and understanding to their clients it is not surprising that they also tend to see this as part of the solicitor's role; 26% saw the solicitor as providing guidance and feedback in relation to the court and its procedures; 15% saw the solicitor as providing support for frightened and unsure clients. As was mentioned above this is not an aspect of their role which solicitors tend to discuss. This does not necessarily mean that solicitors are unaware of their support functions. However the total absence of any discussion of client relationships in the training of most solicitors suggests that this may not be an element in their thinking about their role. Some social workers (15%) specifically mention the failure of solicitors to be supportive to their clients, describing them as detached, unsympathetic and treating cases simply as a matter of business.

Apart from telephone calls prior to the hearing, the main contact between social workers and solicitors occurs around the court and it is largely during the court hearing itself when social workers can see the solicitor performing his role. About one fifth of social workers think that solicitors do a good job in court, another fifth are unimpressed with what they see but the majority comment on the variability between solicitors. Criticisms centre on the apparent inexperience of solicitors or their ignorance of child care cases. Solicitors were also thought to be badly prepared. There is a particular concern that solicitors 'crib' their information from the social worker.

In summary, social workers generally subscribe to the concept of legal representation being of benefit to both children and parents. However their ideas on the nature of the advantage or the role of the representative are often vague and frequently conflicted. In general they are unaware of the complexities involved in representing a child and do not realise the difficulties which may confront a solicitor attempting to carry out the role. They observe the variations in the performance of solicitors who they see operating in the court. But by and large they do not have enough experience of going to court to be able to sort out the relative contribution of personal skills, role definitions and case circumstances which determine a solicitor's performance in a particular case. Their attitudes seem to be mainly determined by their most

recent experience or by notorious cases either of their own or of their colleagues. These attitudes can be completely changed by the advent of a new case. Such transformations in the attitudes of social workers to particular solicitors were observed in a number of instances during the course of the study. Solicitors previously highly thought of by an area office for the effective presentation of cases were suddenly deemed unprofessional and untrustworthy when a case arose in which they equally effectively opposed the local authority case. Social workers often depend on each other for their working attitudes both to individual solicitors and to solicitors generally. Experiences of a dramatic kind frequently achieve the status of office myths without any checking of the circumstances in which they arose.

Role relationships between private solicitors and social workers

Social workers may come into contact with private solicitors when representation is being obtained for the child or the parent, during the preparation of the case for court or at the court on the day the case is being heard. The relationship between the two professional groups can be looked at in the context of these three separate phases.

1. Obtaining representation

The confusion which results from the fact that the child and not the parent is the party to the proceedings and therefore entitled to representation, extends not only to the role of the representative but to the way in which representation is obtained. The parent or guardian may approach a solicitor on behalf of the child. If the child is legally aided and there is judged to be a conflict of interest between the parent and the child then the court may appoint a solicitor. (R. v. Northampton Justices, ex parte McElkennon, 1976.120 S.J. 677). In the larger courts with several courtrooms running simultaneously hearing the full range of juvenile cases there is usually a duty solicitor scheme in operation. In practice this means that the solicitors who are attending court for other cases may be contacted directly or at the request of the court. Obtaining representation in this way happens occasionally in care cases but is unlikely to be of much benefit to the child unless it occurs at the stage of an interim order. Then the solicitor would have time to prepare the case. In default of parents obtaining a solicitor for the child or the court ordering representation, it often falls to social workers to take some part in the matter and there is considerable variation in practice.

Many social workers do no more than advise their clients as to the right of the child to be represented. When the child is young no further action may be taken and the child is not represented unless the parents make the arrangements. As indicated by the one authority in which social workers took no active part in obtaining representation, parents are likely to do this in about a third of cases. With older children or when the social worker is not entirely convinced of the need for a care order in a case, the social worker may be more active in getting representation for the child, perhaps contacting a solicitor on

his behalf and taking the child to see him. This situation largely arises in non-school attendance or criminal cases. In cases where the child has been removed from home on a place of safety order or an interim care order has been obtained then it is open to the local authority acting *in loco parentis* to arrange representation. The extent to which this is done seems to reflect a feedback process from the courts. Some courts wish to see the child being represented and area offices relating to those courts usually have a well developed practice. Only one area office had a clear policy that the child should be represented. When the local authority acts to obtain representation for a child in its care, practice varies from one area to another; a representative of the department may simply sign the legal aid form and the court may then nominate and contact a solicitor, either known to them as handling these kind of cases or from a duty rota. In other cases the social worker or courts officer may suggest a solicitor or have made contact with a solicitor to see if he is able to take the case. The legal aid form naming the solicitor may be filled out either by the local authority or the court.

For social workers to take an active part in obtaining the services of a particular solicitor they would need to know the names of appropriate people to contact; 71% of social workers interviewed said that they did know appropriate solicitors either by personal contact, by seeing them in court, by reputation or a list held in the area office. 29% said they did not know anyone suitable. The knowledge of particular solicitors is strongly determined by the amount of court experience of particular social workers and the frequency of representation of children in the local juvenile court. Local practice also affects the pattern of work as it comes to private solicitors; 26% said that all or most cases in which they represent the child come to them from social services; 28% all or most come from contact being made by parents; 6% from the court or a rota scheme and 32% from a mixture of sources. The interlocking nature of the local practice can be highlighted by contrasting two authorities:

Authority 1: In this authority the local juvenile court does not take an active stance on representation for children and representation is relatively infrequent; social workers do not obtain representation for the child using their powers *in loco parentis;* a large number of social workers (40%) would not know a suitable solicitor to contact; and 8/10 solicitors said their cases come by contact made by the parents.

Authority 4: In this authority there are three juvenile courts operating different policies. In the largest court the magistrates want to see the child represented and the courts officer in the area office takes an active part in obtaining the services of particular solicitors. In a second court a rota scheme is in operation. In the third court the clerk is 'against unnecessary representation' and may refuse legal aid for the child when he feels that there is no conflict of interest with the parents. Nearly all (94%) social workers in the authority said that they knew or knew of a suitable solicitor. Six of the ten solicitors interviewed in the authority area said that all or most of their work representing children came from contact made through the social services offices and two more said that some of their cases were obtained in this way.

The extent to which social workers should be involved in obtaining representation for a child when the social services are bringing the case to court is a matter of some debate. Parents often make no arrangements for the representation of the child and they may not know a suitable person to contact. The child is more likely to be represented by a solicitor with experience in the field if the social workers make the arrangements. They are also likely to involve a solicitor early in the proceedings rather than just before the case comes to court. If the solicitor is approached by the parents it may lead to confusion both for them and for the solicitor as to whom he is representing. The solicitor's responsibility to represent the child may be clearer if he is contacted by the social services. It may also be the case that if a social worker has obtained the service for a child of a particular solicitor he may be more predisposed to cooperate with that solicitor over providing information than if the solicitor was obtained by the parents.

The principal disadvantage of social services being active in naming a particular solicitor is that this may be thought to undermine the independent role the solicitor should play. Some social workers felt it would be unethical for them to obtain a solicitor for the child. In the first place the social services might be tempted to nominate a solicitor who they think will be sympathetic to their point of view. This does not need to happen consciously but may be implicit in their concept of what constitutes a 'good' solicitor. Pressures may also be felt by the solicitor if a substantial proportion of his work comes from the social services department. A few solicitors showed some awareness of this potential danger although they felt that their professional ethics were an adequate guarantee of independence. The practice may also contribute to the feeling of the parents that they are excluded and that their rights as parents have been effectively removed well before the case comes to court.

On balance it is probably undesirable for the social services to take any part in naming or contacting a solicitor in any case in which they are the applicant in the proceedings. Where they are responsible for the child under a place of safety or interim care order they should see that the child does obtain representation by contacting the court and signing the legal aid form. However the court should be totally independent in its choice of solicitor preferably from a rota system, kept under regular review, of solicitors working in the field. The parents should be informed by the court of the solicitor who will be representing the child. The exclusion of the parents from the proceedings cannot be further dealt with except by making them party to the proceedings and granting them legal aid.

2. Preparation of the case

Most solicitors see the social worker as an important source of information in the preparation of the case; 44/50 said they would contact the social worker when preparing a case; 82% of social workers said they had contact with a solicitor prior to a hearing and 83% said they would be prepared to contact a solicitor who they knew was acting in a case. Many social workers however express reservations about talking to solicitors about cases; 21% said they would discuss the case freely, 17% said they would confine themselves to facts,

but 51% said they would be reticent and reluctant to talk freely. Many of this latter group specifically commented that 'you have to be careful what you say to solicitors because they may use the information against you'. A third of social workers felt that their response to the request for information would depend on the case and whether they knew and trusted the solicitor involved. A few distinguished between a solicitor representing the child and one representing the parents but this was not a major consideration, perhaps because of the comparative rarity of the latter.

In relation to the report prepared by the social worker for the court, 32% of social workers said they would give the solicitor a copy, 15% that they would tell him what they were going to say and 43% that they would not give him a copy or convey the contents. Attitudes on this practice varied somewhat between the authorities: Authorities 2 and 4 were more in favour of giving the solicitor the report (52% and 45% respectively) and in Authority 3 more social workers were against the practice (57%). Somewhat surprisingly attitudes of social workers to the way they should relate to solicitors do not vary with age, experience, qualification or familiarity with courts.

The reluctance of many social workers to provide information and documentary evidence is reflected in the experience of solicitors. Some have sufficiently close relationships with the local area office that they are provided with full access to all relevant documents and background information. About half the solicitors interviewed felt they could obtain adequate documentation in relation to a case although only a quarter obtained a copy of the social enquiry report, often just before going into court. Half the solicitors said they had sufficient opportunity to discuss possible compromise with the social services before the case came to court. However a significant proportion of solicitors (16/50) felt that their preparation of cases was, on occasions, impaired by lack of information from the social services. A few felt that the problem was so severe that they often were 'going into court blind' with little or no idea of the relevant considerations in the case.

Much of the difficulty experienced by solicitors centres around the availability of the social enquiry report because of its importance both as a full résumé of the background and the influence it has in court. (A full discussion of the nature, status and use of the SER will be included later in the discussion of court hearings.) Disclosure of documents is a bone of contention in many areas of law, particularly criminal law, and the same arguments arise in care proceedings. The solicitor representing the defendant or respondent argues that because of the prosecution's or applicant's responsibility to prove his case he should be obliged to reveal his case beforehand to give the respondent an opportunity to check his information. The authority bringing the case argues that he should not be obliged to reveal his case, that information he provides can be misused by the other side and that it is up to the respondent to make his own investigations. This latter argument fails to recognise the discrepancy between the resources available to government authorities and those available to solicitors to make such investigations. The attitudes of social workers and policemen to private solicitors are rather similar in this respect; both groups tend to feel resentful that they have done all the groundwork and see solicitors as simply making use of their efforts. Solicitors on the other hand argue that

there should be disclosure of documents as part of the open process of law. It is argued that on some occasions proceedings could be shortened and speeded up if both sides could agree many relevant facts before the court hearing. The practice of disclosing documents and agreeing much of the background is seen as an advantage of proceedings in the high court.

One important part of the decision processes from which all private solicitors seem to be excluded is the case conference. Neither solicitors nor social workers seemed to have seriously considered whether a solicitor representing the child should attend such events. There are some difficulties: solicitors mentioned that they might not have time, they would not be paid to attend and that the conference might occur before they were instructed. There may also be problems of confidentiality and several solicitors thought they would be exposed to information that they could not use and would have to keep from their clients. Some solicitors however recognised the importance of the case conference as the effective decision-making machinery in child care cases. They argued that there was little they could effectively do to represent the child if they did not attend these important events. In particular a few mentioned case conferences held after a court hearing to decide on the placement of the child.

One issue not raised by solicitors and of which they are unlikely to be aware is that since case conferences need to operate a consensus mode of decision-making they would be subject to strong co-option pressures which might undermine their independence.

Despite specific difficulties in obtaining information from social services most solicitors felt that they received reasonable co-operation from social workers (20 said good co-operation, 17 reasonable) although some mentioned having difficulty with young or inexperienced social workers (7). Co-operation is seen as depending in large part on the development of local personal relationships. Lack of co-operation, when it does occur, seems to have three main components.

(a) *Uncertainty/anxiety*. Solicitors perceive social workers' uncertainties and anxieties about care proceedings particularly among the less experienced. They report that ignorance of the law, procedures and the legal significance of certain matters contribute to social workers' unwillingness to talk to them as well as a more general attitude of distrust and suspicion. The lack of clarity about what information is relevant to communicate and does not breach confidentiality seems to be an underlying problem in ease of communication from social workers to solicitors.

(b) *Understanding of roles*. 29/50 solicitors felt that social workers did not understand their role in care proceedings. Some went further and argued that the lack of understanding derived from a failure to accept the role of the court and consequently the solicitor's role in court hearings. Social workers are seen as so involved in the case and the decision to remove a child from its family that they cannot see that there might be another view of the matter or that an independent review of the facts may not accord with their assessment. It may of course be unreasonable to expect social workers to see the matter in any other way since they are trying to act in what they see as the best interests of

63

their clients. On the other hand some social workers also feel that solicitors do not understand the social worker's role and do not know what they do.

(c) *Polarisation*. The basically adversarial nature of court hearings inevitably creates a degree of polarisation between the parties. Each side sees the other as determined to 'win' and adopting attitudes and behaviour appropriate to conflict not co-operation; 10 solicitors saw the failure to achieve co-operation as resulting from polarisation (social workers have made up their minds, won't consider other alternatives or views, are only concerned to win, see solicitors as only concerned to win and to do them down). Social workers also have an underlying stereotype of solicitors that they are only concerned with winning (23%), are only concerned with legalities (41%) and short-term concerns (18%).

To achieve limited and specific co-operation in the context of the conflict model of operation implicit in adversarial proceedings requires a highly developed and structured understanding of the roles involved and the status of different classes of information. Solicitors develop such role definitions in their relationships with each other but no parallel understanding exists for social workers in their relationship with solicitors. Solicitors can and do also contact the solicitor for the local authority in the preparation of a case (44/50 said they would do so and most said they find the solicitor helpful). (It would of course, be a breach of professional etiquette for solicitors to criticise each other's performance.) The established role relationships between solicitors is illustrated by the fact that 14/50 said they would prefer to deal with the local authority solicitor rather than social workers. The shared language, knowledge and methods of operating was specifically mentioned by 6 solicitors and 6 said they found the solicitor more willing to talk about the case. 15 said they would speak to both as they have different functions and 14 said they would prefer to deal with the social worker, emphasising that the social worker is the one with the information about the case. The social worker's uncertainty about what information should be conveyed may, on occasions, work to the solicitor's advantage. On the basis of a personal contact he may obtain more information than he would extract from a professional colleague.

3. The court hearing

Most of the face-to-face contact between solicitors and social workers occurs in and around the court hearing. Prior contact is usually restricted to letters and phone calls. Social workers were asked about their perceptions of the attitudes solicitors had to them when they had contact in a case; 17% felt solicitors were friendly, cooperative and helpful; 25% said that solicitors value and appreciate the job social workers do and respect social workers; 20% expressed neutral views, they are reasonable, tolerate us; and 20% felt the attitudes were negative (we are not regarded as equal, they patronise us, social workers are seen as do-gooders, interfering, and we are not respected). These latter replies raise the question of how the differential status accorded to these two professions affects their interactions. An analysis of the public image of the two groups and their own attitudes to their professions suggest that solicitors are not only accorded higher status than social workers but also have

greater self-confidence in their professional standing. Social workers recognise this discrepancy in their stereotype of solicitors: 14% mention status factors such as middle class, conservative, better paid, and 23% mention that solicitors are in an established profession with a defined role. The issue is particularly likely to emerge in the setting of the court itself. The court is essentially the solicitor's home-ground, with which he is familiar and in which his status is assured. Some social workers specifically mentioned that at court the social workers' role is seen as secondary by solicitors and stopping at the court door. This sense of exclusion was also noted above in the social workers' feelings about the social character of the court.

The social worker's role in court has become increasingly important as the juvenile court has given greater attention to the overall welfare of the child. Thus it might be supposed that the status balance may have tipped in favour of the social workers. Anderson (1978) studied two juvenile courts and reported that in the court with a strong welfare orientation the status of the social workers was high in comparison with the solicitors. In the more traditional court the balance was felt to be the other way round. Solicitors interviewed in our study however did not in general feel that they were treated any differently in the juvenile court as compared to the adult magistrates court. One said that he did feel like an intruder when he was excluded from the court when an earlier case was being heard, and one said he thought social workers were given priority.

In the courtroom both social workers and solicitors have an opportunity to observe the performance of the other in public. Social workers are not particularly impressed by solicitors in court and many comment on the variability between solicitors (47%). Solicitors also observe variability in social workers' performance as witnesses which they see as depending on experience. About one third of solicitors are critical of social workers' performance and particularly commented on the role confusions which arise, for example, social workers mix up fact and opinion in giving evidence and are prone to use hearsay. A few noted that what is required in court is different from the social worker's normal job. In particular, the court requires the social worker to express his opinions orally in response to very structured questions and to confine his answers to what he was asked about. He must also respond to challenges to his opinions when he is cross-examined.

Despite the constant theme of good personal contact between solicitors and social workers as being an important factor in communication and cooperation very few of either group mentioned better contact as an improvement they would like to see in the system. Somewhat more importance was placed on the need for specialised training and experience both for themselves and for the other group.

Chapter IV Legal proceedings in child care cases

In this chapter the sample of cases included in the study are described. First, the characteristics of the families and children who were involved in the cases are summarised. This provides an overall picture of the kinds of families and family problems with which the agencies and the courts have to deal. Since the data on families was collected from files, interviews, reports for the court, etc. the findings reflect the perception of the families by the agencies rather than a first hand appraisal of the families and their circumstances by the research team. This point is of greater importance the more subjective the assessment involved, for example, whether or not the family is homeless is probably more reliable data than whether the relationship between the parent and the child is disturbed.

Second, the decision phase of the process is considered; the circumstances in which the decision to take proceedings was made, how the case was defined in terms of the legal proceedings, and the role of external agencies in the decision (particularly the police and education departments). Case conferences are considered in this context. Once the decision to proceed is made then the case is prepared for court. This pre-hearing phase is described with particular reference to its length, why delays seem to occur and what happens to the children during this period. The relationships between the social worker, the legal department and the private solicitors during this phase is also discussed.

The cases which came to court are then considered. Since the majority of cases in the sample were care proceedings, this section concentrates on hearings in juvenile courts. High court hearings are discussed towards the end of the chapter, particularly using them for comparison with the juvenile courts on aspects of practice and procedure.

The juvenile courts are first looked at in physical terms. The physical environment of the courts are important in care proceedings. The surroundings can constrain and determine social interactions. The environment and the atmosphere of the court also are signs to the participants of the significance and importance of what is happening. The procedures and practices of the courts, the parts played by the various role holders and the overall pattern of case hearings are then described. The roles and relationships of the solicitors and social workers in the cases studied are also discussed.

The circumstance of the children and families involved in cases

1. The children

In child care cases action may be taken which affects more than one child in

the household. In the sample of 72 cases studied 15 involved more than one child and 91 children were directly concerned. Action is normally taken against more than one child when there is thought to be some risk of injury or neglect. This was the case in 13 of the 15 cases involving more than one child. (Not all cases where there is an element of risk involve all the children in a household becoming the subject of proceedings. In some cases the risk is only thought to affect one child.)

Other children are also indirectly implicated in the cases. In 15 of the 72 families other children of the family were already in the care of the local authority, thus involving an additional 34 children. In 26 families children other than those who were the subject of the proceedings were living in the household (60 additional children). Thus in total 185 children were involved in the cases in some way.

Of the 91 children who were the subject of proceedings 43 were boys and 48 were girls. Twenty were under the age of one year, 17 were between 1 and 5, 20 between 5 and 10 and 32 were over ten years. Each age group was fairly evenly divided between boys and girls. The grounds used in care prodeedings tend to relate to particular age or sex groups. Young children of both sexes are nearly always involved in care proceedings under the proper development grounds (S.1.2.a) or b) CYPA 1969). Occasionally wardship proceedings are invoked in relation to a baby who is still in hospital. Amongst younger children boys are equally as often involved in these cases as girls. Proper development grounds are also sometimes used for girls between 5 and 10 years of age. Ground c) 'moral danger' is only used for girls and principally in relation to girls between 5 and 10. Few boys in this age group were involved in any of the cases. The care proceedings grounds beyond control (d) and education (e) largely apply to older children. Similarly criminal prosecutions are only brought against older children. In the older age group boys are more frequently involved in criminal cases or care proceedings on education grounds. Girls are more often involved in beyond control cases.

2. The families

In the majority of cases (63/72) it is, or it is assumed to be, the mother who has or is claiming care of the child. In 7 cases a single father was the main contender for case of the child. It is fairly rare (10 cases) for there to be more than one person or household available to care for the child. Sometimes grandparents, separated fathers or other relatives are considered as possible alternatives.

Many of the families whose children become the subject of proceedings have characteristics which might make it more difficult for them to cope with caring for a child.

Of the 72 families
- 36 were single parent families;
- in 33 the main provider for the household was unemployed;
- in 18 a parent was mentally ill, alcoholic or a drug abuser;
- 14 involved unstable relationships, co-habitees, etc.;
- 10 were homeless;

- in 7 the parent was physically handicapped;
- 7 were single fathers;
- 6 were immigrant families;
- 5 were mentally handicapped.

A number of the families had more than one of these characteristics. In fact 9 families had 4 or more; 13 had three, 23 had two, 15 had one and only 12 of the 72 had none of these features.

These characteristics may not only impede a family's ability to cope with caring for a child, they are also the kinds of characteristics which are likely to bring a family to the attention of the social services. The family may themselves seek help from welfare services, or more attention may be paid to them. For example, a family with very poor housing standards may be visited more frequently by health visitors. Many of the families had been known to the social services department for some time: 31 had been known for more than 5 years; 19 for 1 to 5 years and only 13 appear to have been unknown before the need for the proceedings arose.

The families whose children become the subject of proceedings are mainly deprived working class families. 66 of the families were classified as D or E on the socio-economic status scale. It is rare for middle class families to be involved in care or related proceedings; 3 were classified as A, B or C_1 and 5 as C_2.

When the decision to apply for the care of a child is being considered by the local authority, for instance at a case conference, a number of considerations or factors are repeatedly referred to. From examining social work files, attending case conferences and hearing evidence in court we developed a classification of these factors as a means of recording the factors considered in a decision. Table III gives the classification and the frequency with which these factors were mentioned in the sample of cases. The factors often involve subjective judgments or assessments. The findings cannot therefore be used as providing a reliable description of the problems of the families. The classification does however reflect how the cases were seen and presented.

Table III Classification of Features of Families or Children Involved in Care Cases

CHILDREN   N
1. Risk of physical harm to the child.

		N
– child physically damaged		16
– failure to thrive		6
– parent has violent tendencies		27
– parent provides inadequate physical care		31
Any one of these		44

2. Child is committing criminal offences or is behaving in an extremely anti-social way.   16

CHILDREN   N
  3. Child is showing problems at
     school.

                                 – performance very poor   9
                                   – attendance very poor   18

                                   Any one of these   24

  4. Child is showing developmental or
     behavioural problems.

                                   – behavioural problems at home   19
                                   – child aggressive, unmanageable 17
                                   – child's peer group relationships are
                                      disturbed   12
                                   – child is failing to develop
                                      emotionally   9
                                   – child is failing to develop cognitively 3

                                   Any one of these   25

FAMILY/HOME
  5. Poor material circumstances in the
     home.

                                   – insufficient income   18
                                   – excessive or inappropriate
                                      expenditure   8
                                   – lack of basic amenities   7

                                   Any one of these   26

  6. Parents' incompetence.

                                   – in physically caring for the child 31
                                   – in housekeeping, cleanliness, etc. 16
                                   – in managing money   8

                                   Any one of these   35

  7. Instability, uncertainty,
     unpredictability of home and familiy
     situation.   25

  8. Morality or criminality of parents.

                                   – either parent has history of
                                      criminality   14
                                   – sexual or moral deviance of parent 6

                                   Any one of these   17

  9. Relationship between parent and
     child unsatisfactory.

                                   – lack of control or discipline   26
                                   – disturbed or unsatisfactory
                                      relationship   20
                                   – lack of affection for the child 11

                                   Any one of these   42

10. Relationship between the parents
     stressed or disturbed.   18

A number of these considerations in relation to the child's need for care and the ability of the family to provide it are mentioned in most cases. In general the factors relating to children provide the prima facie reasons for intervention and reflect the main grounds which are laid down as a basis for an application under S.1. CYPA 1969. The family and home circumstances are normally recorded as subsidiary arguments for intervention and relate to the 'care and control' test in care proceedings or the relevance of a care order. It should however be noted that this analysis of the reason for taking proceedings introduces a more systematic approach than is normally apparent in records or discussions of individual cases. In addition, this information may not all be available at the time the decision to apply for an order is taken; it may only emerge as data is collected for the court hearing.

The decision to take proceedings

In many cases the decision to take proceedings is made under crisis conditions. Alternatively a crisis occurs in which action has to be taken immediately and this constitutes a *de facto* decision. In 42 cases a crisis situation appeared to exist at the start of the decision phase. In 44 cases a place of safety order was taken and the child removed from home or the parent prevented from removing the child to its home. In these crises the child was often thought to be in physical danger (32 cases) or the parents appeared to be unable to provide adequate physical care. A crisis can occur when a child is clearly in need and someone must take action to see he is cared for. Thus a child may be found to be damaged or failing to develop physically; a child may be born in a family where other children have been non-accidentally injured or inadequately cared for; a child may have run away and be found wandering in the streets; or a child may be abandoned. In other cases, however, there are more subjective assessments operating in the definition of the situation as a 'crisis', e.g. unsatisfactory relationships between the child and the parent (14); moral or criminal behaviour of the parent (14); unstable or unpredictable home environment (23). The 'crisis' may be defined or even created by people such as parents, teachers, neighbours, police, etc. if they believe that action should be taken. In some situations a decision may have been made at a case conference or meeting that a place of safety order should be taken if any further event or change occurs.

In other cases the situation had apparently been deteriorating over a period of time (25 cases) and at some point a decision was made to take legal proceedings. These cases tended to be those where the child's behaviour (criminal (10), school (12) or behaviour problems (14)) was the main source of concern. The behaviour itself may have become more severe, or other strategies for dealing with it may have been tried and failed.

Even though the decision to remove the child and to take a place of safety order may be made in response to an immediate need to protect the child, subsequent considerations of the case may suggest that legal proceedings are not necessary. However this only occurred in 2/44 cases when a place of safety order was taken. Thus applying for a place of safety order is normally the effective decision point in a case.

It was suggested in the description of the decision-making process at the beginning of the last chapter that the decision to apply for a care order comprises two elements: the child's need for care and the capacity of the local authority to supply that need. However as far as could be judged from records, only in 8 cases was resource provision an explicit issue in the decision whether or not to take proceedings. In 24 cases there was some indication that placement had been planned before the case came to court. In cases where the 'need' for care element is very strong the resource issues tend to be taken for granted. However in cases where the child's behaviour is the principle reason for action then the resource provision element is obviously more important. In the 22 cases when it was school problems or criminal behaviour that precipitated action resources were an issue in the decision in 5 of the cases, and placement planning was considered in 7. In 10 cases there was no mention of resources throughout the preparation of the case.

The decision to take proceedings involves not only establishing the need for intervention but also whether there are sufficient grounds to take the case to court, which legal procedure is appropriate and who is the responsible agency. That is, the case must be conceived of in legal terms. Changes do occasionally occur at a later date (for example, from care proceedings to wardship) but normally the early decision stands and subsequent case preparation is handled accordingly. Table IV shows the main case types in terms of the classification of circumstances of the child and families.

The table shows clearly how in all kinds of cases there are many relevant factors and no clear-cut equation between family circumstances and legal grounds. In the most numerous 'proper development' cases all the circumstances are mentioned frequently except criminal behaviour and school problems which do not apply since these children are usually very young. The 'all-in' quality of the factors mentioned in these cases may reflect the true complexity of the cases but may also arise from uncertainty about what is relevant to consider under the wide and ill-defined ground of proper development. When the more specific grounds apply as in beyond control, education and criminal cases, the pattern of circumstances is somewhat less dispersed. However even in these cases there is considerable overlap. For example criminal behaviour of the child is a feature both in criminal and in beyond control cases. School problems are a common feature in both these types of cases as well as in education cases. In all these types of cases, not only does the specific ground apply but the more general concern with the failure of the parent/child relationship, in many cases a specific concern about discipline and control.

The decision to take proceedings is frequently made either at an interagency meeting, case conference or discussion, or after consultation between agencies. In only 2 cases could we find no reference to contact with other agencies. In 25 cases the decision to proceed seems to have been largely made within the social services department. Case conferences were held in 48 of the 72 cases and at least 36 of these were closely concerned with the decision to take legal proceedings. Whether or not the case conference is supposed to be a 'decision-making body', the outcomes or minutes of conferences are frequently recorded in decision terms (e.g. 'it was decided to apply for a care order'; 'it was agreed that care proceedings should be begun'). Conferences are more

Table IV Circumstances of Families and Children for Each Type of Legal Proceeding

| Circumstances | Care Proceedings | | | | | Crimi- nal | Ward- ship | S.2 Resol- utions |
	(a) Proper Devel- opment	(b) Same House- hold	(c) Moral Danger	(d) Beyond Control	(e) Edu- cation			
Children								
1. Child at risk	18	7	2	2	1	1	7	3
2. Criminal behaviour	—	—	2	6	2	5	2	—
3. School prob- lems	3	—	1	6	8	2	1	—
4. Developmental or behavioural problems	4	1	1	9	5	5	2	2
Families								
5. Poor material circumstances	10	2	2	2	1	1	4	3
6. Parents' incompetence	14	5	2	1	1	1	6	2
7. Situation unstable	12	7	2	—	—	—	2	1
8. Criminality or morality of parent	6	5	2	—	1	—	2	1
9. Parent-child relationship unsatisfactory	9	4	3	7	6	5	4	2
10. Parents' relationship disturbed	10	2	1	—	1	1	1	1
Other chil- dren in care	4	7	1	1	1	—	4	—
Total cases	33	7	3	9	8	5	9	3

frequently held in cases when there is an element of risk (25/30 cases where grounds (a) or (b) applied). They were held in only half of all other cases. This difference reflects the recommendations of the procedural guidelines for non-accidental injury cases. (The membership of these conferences are described below).

Among the agencies who participate with the social services in deciding whether an application should be made to take a child into care the most notable are the police and the education department. Like the social services and to a limited extent the NSPCC both agencies have statutory responsibilities; the education department for school attendance and certain

aspects of the child's behaviour at school; and the police for the prevention and detection of crime and for bringing those responsible for criminal acts to justice. Both these agencies have a measure of discretion as to the exercise of their power although the discretion tends to diminish as the subject of it becomes more significant. Thus the police frequently chose not to prosecute children caught pilfering but they have no discretion over whether or not to prosecute in cases of murder, incest, GBH or serious sexual assault.

Police and Social Services

Since the CYPA 1969 the police have been under considerable pressure to revise their view of the exercise of discretion about the prosecution of children and young persons and about how to cope with some kinds of criminal acts of parents against their children. The police now actively consider the argument against prosecution. In so doing they need to consider and often accept arguments either raised by social workers or deriving from social work theory. While it is claimed that the police have always exercised the obvious social welfare component of their role, all the officers interviewed in connection with the study[1] named the 1969 Act as the turning point for a growth in the weight given to welfare arguments in the decision whether or not to prosecute. They also emphasised the significance of liaison with social services in promoting understanding of and respect for social work methods and theory.

Given the autonomy of the 43 police forces in the UK it is not surprising that when considered in detail each force has its own way of relating to social service departments, its own liaison machinery and its own special kind of adaptation to the spirit of the 1969 Act. The development of the relationship has not been easy: a hard case, a discordant personal relationship or a liaison device falling into disrepute can destroy credibility and trust over night. However it is felt that working relationships are now more stable and productive than five years ago and that setbacks can be more easily handled. In some places the development of liaison between police officers and social services has depended on personal relationships between senior members of the agencies. In others there has been a greater reliance on carefully defined procedures and agreed criteria upon which decisions are made. In Authority 5 where there is the greatest emphasis on formal relationships between police and social workers at all levels, there is also a formal machinery involving a weekly juvenile liaison meeting to discuss specific cases and general issues. This double indemnity is a response to the juvenile problems encountered in that area. (The police area for the authority includes a large metropolitan area). The juvenile liaison bureau system in London represents the most developed and systematic mode of handling juveniles with senior officers

---

[1] The material reported here is based on interviews with the senior officers with responsibility for children in each of the non-London police forces. In the London local authority the liaison with social services is handled through the Juvenile Liaison Bureau. The Community Relations Branch, New Scotland Yard, has overall police responsibility for the scheme in the Metropolitan Police and the scheme was discussed with this branch. Information on more local relationships is not therefore available for the London authority.

responsible for decisions about cautioning, interagency liaison and NAI cases. The volume of juvenile crime and the mobility of young people within the metropolitan area have required the development of a more integrated approach.

Officers feel that they have access to those case conferences in which they have a role to play. The case conference and the area review committees are seen as effective parts of the liaison machinery although the area review committee does not often deal with issues with which the police are directly concerned. The degree to which senior officers want to be involved in case conferences seems to be related to the presence or absence of a previous history of exclusion. Where the police feel they have in the past been excluded the tendency is to want to be involved in all case conferences as a matter of course. Where there has been long-standing co-operation these officers are happy to be asked to attend only those conferences in which they are directly involved in the cases. In Authority 3 the officer with NAI responsibility said he only wanted to go to cases where criminal activity was involved. He didn't consider neglect fell into this category. In Authorities 2 and 4 on the other hand it was particularly important to the officers concerned that they were not excluded. The level of satisfaction concerning the administration and working of case conferences seemed to be generally high. No force reported any problems with length of notice for meetings, receipt of relevant information, meeting procedure, quality of the minutes, etc.

Although there are differences of emphasis, the procedures for dealing with NAI and juvenile crime cases are essentially the same. Unless discovery of an NAI case is prompted by a domestic disturbance or complaint to the police, initial information about NAI cases comes from the social services to the divisional officer responsible. Considering the circumstances and severity of the injuries etc., he will investigate with a view to possible prosecution. In their crime prevention role the police will also be concerned to ensure that no further injuries are inflicted on the child. They may take a place of safety order or take individual parents into custody and bail them on condition they do not return to the family home. In making decisions about prosecuting in NAI cases Authority 2 refers all such decisions to assistant chief constable level. Authorities 3 and 4 operate fairly strictly according to the severity of injury using normal distinctions between common assault, ABH and GBH or wounding. Authority 5 responds to each case on its merits with considerable open-mindedness by the senior officer to social arguments. There were no complaints made about the effectiveness of inter-agency communication over non-accidental injury cases in general, although spokesmen for 3 forces commented on the lack of cover after office hours in large local authority areas.

In dealing with juveniles the police made a move from specialists to generalists which paralleled that in social work. In response to pressures to reduce the restriction of women to certain job types in the police, police women tended to move away from specialising in family and juvenile matters (although two of the officers interviewed were women). This meant an overall loss in specialist knowledge in the area. In some forces the absence of real expertise was commented on. In Authority 2 the liaison officer particularly

regretted the loss of specialists in dealing with complex family situations and felt that this could on occasions contribute to poor communication with social workers. In London the recognition of the loss was important in the decision to set up the juvenile liaison bureaux. In the other metropolitan authority considerable efforts were made to establish and maintain communication with social workers through liaison meetings and local contact with residential beat officers.

Juvenile crime and the decision to prosecute or caution is dealt with at the local station (sub-divisional) level or in London at juvenile bureaux. Formal cautions, usually carried out at weekends by an inspector or a more senior officer in full uniform with the offender and his parents attending the police station, are now commonly used for first offenders. Indeed in Authority 2 it is common to caution re-offenders. In Authority 3 cautioning depends on the type of offence rather than on the juvenile's 'record'. In Authority 5 the weekly cautioning sessions are attended by a social worker (on a roster basis). This practice is both valuable for maintaining liaison between the agencies and provides a useful point of contact with a family. Of all the issues covered in interviews with police officers, the cautioning of juveniles produced the widest range of views. In Authority 5 officers prefer to treat each case on its merits; in Authority 3 rules and criteria are preferred and Authority 2 try to assess whether or not the juvenile is 'out of control' (a global criterion relating to the CYPA 1969). Officers also disagree in their view of the efficacy of cautioning. Although effectiveness is clearly important to them, none of them could quote statistics from their own force or others to indicate whether the practice was worthwhile.

Police and social work definitions of criminality were discussed but police officers generally discounted the notion that there are major differences in view. Obvious points of friction were unlawful sexual intercourse, non-serious incestuous assault, possession of stolen property and minor pilfering. None of the forces suggested that the differences in attitude to criminality caused practical problems when the agencies consulted each other about a particular case. Two forces commented on the attitudes of juvenile court clerks to juvenile crime. The police in some areas are under pressure from the courts to cut down the liaison time with social services and thereby speed up the process of bringing juveniles to court. As research findings indicate that the court appearance itself and its proximity to the criminal act are the prime factors in deterrence, this pressure appears to be warranted. However juvenile liaison officers are well aware of the pressures on social service departments and do not feel that they want to make an issue of the time liaison takes.

Social workers also come into contact with the police when they act as the third party in 'lieu' of parents during interrogation of juveniles by the CID or uniformed branch. There were no adverse comments on the way in which social workers discharged their duty except again that often it was difficult to obtain the services of a social worker, especially the relevant caseworker, out of office hours and at short notice.

Police Involvement in the Decision on Cases

The police were involved in some way in 45 cases. In 13 cases the child was

known or thought to be committing criminal offences. These children were usually presenting other problems such as poor school attendance, behaviour problems, running away from home, tension with parents, or inability of parents to control the child. The police, social services and the education department were all therefore involved. Despite apparently similar backgrounds to these cases they were dealt with legally in different ways: in five cases the police prosecuted for criminal offences and the social services then recommended a care order. In 7 cases the social services applied for a care order, 5 on 'beyond control' grounds and 2 on grounds of 'moral danger'. In 1 case the education department took care proceedings under the 'education' condition of the 1969 Act.

There are no obvious differences between the cases in the nature of the family background. This is not surprising since a care order is only likely to be recommended if the background of the child is disturbed. In a few cases the definition of the cases seems to be a matter of legal rules or convenience. One case involved a child who was repeatedly offending but who could not be prosecuted as she was under 10. A care order was applied for by the local authority on grounds of her being in 'moral danger'. In another case, the child was already in voluntary care. A criminal prosecution was therefore more appropriate than care proceedings. In a third case the education department was applying for a care order. Subsequently the police prosecuted the child for an offence and a care order was sought at this hearing rather than waiting for a later court date. The cases are also distinguished by sex; 4 out of the 5 criminal cases involved boys and 6 out of 7 'beyond control' or 'moral danger' cases involved girls.

In criminal cases the offences involved were, or are at least were seen to be, more serious in police terms. They were presented as more essentially 'criminal' in nature, e.g. arson, theft, criminal damage. The family had usually been known to the social services for some time but the situation was not serious enough to require intervention. Other voluntary measures may have been tried and failed or some new element may have been introduced into the situation (e.g. breakdown of placement, victimisation by peer group) which justifies the need to take legal action at this time. In 'beyond control' cases the criminal activities were seen more as a nuisance than essentially criminal in kind, e.g. pilfering from home or school, unlawful sexual intercourse. In 3 cases the children were not previously known to the social services and were referred to them by the police. Once they had been referred (e.g. by police taking a place of safety order on a child who was sleeping rough) the social services then took care proceedings. (With relatively minor offences of this kind and little or no criminal record, the juvenile court would be unlikely to make a care order if the cases were taken on a criminal prosecution).

The legal definition of a case which involves criminal behaviour of the child thus seems to result from a mixture of administrative considerations and how the case is perceived. The third contributing factor is the nature of local liaison. Case conferences were held in 7 of the 13 cases and the police were recorded as having attended only one of these. The liaison with the police is often confined to the formal notification system, perhaps backed up with

telephone calls. In Authority 5 the decisions are made in the weekly liaison meetings between the police and the social services and in Authority 4 (city area) the courts officer has regular meetings with the police at which joint decisions are made. In the authorities where liaison is more formal, the way the case is defined is more predictable from the responsibilities of the agencies. That is, the police will prosecute if the criminal activity justifies doing so. In authorities with close liaison the decision may be made by joint agreement as to the easiest way of achieving an agreed outcome.

The police are also involved in cases when the child is injured or neglected. Out of the 30 cases in the sample in which the grounds for care proceedings were either proper development or neglect of the child (S.1.2 grounds (a) or (b)) the police were involved in the initiating crisis or event in 18 instances. In some cases the police were the first to be concerned, having been called by a member of the public. In others they took action after being notified by another agency, e.g. NSPCC, duty officer of the social services, hospital, etc., in accordance with NAI procedures, or they made investigations after a case conference. In the 13 cases where a child had suffered physical harm, a case conference was held in each case and the police attended 11 (in one case the conference membership was not recorded). It is apparently less common to invite the police to conferences in cases where the child has not been damaged but is thought to be 'at risk'. In only 3 out of the 12 cases of this type did police attend a case conference; in these 3 cases the parents were known to the police or had been recently arrested for other offences. In 7 of the 13 cases involving damage to a child the police brought separate prosecutions against one or both parents.

Considering police involvement in the sample of cases as a whole, the proportion of cases in which the police were concerned in the precipitating event was roughly the same for the five authorities (considering only cases where the police are involved at all). In all, the police initiated action in 25 out of 45 cases in which they are involved at any stage. However civil legal activity by the police (place of safety orders and interim care orders) was more frequent in Authority 2 than in the other areas. In 9 cases out of 45 evenly spread across the five authorities the police were specifically requested to 'do the dirty work' such as sorting out violent arguments, providing a show of authority or dealing with potentially dangerous situations.

Education Department Involvement in Decisions on Cases

In a parallel way to the police, the education department has statutory responsibilities in relation to the child's school behaviour and particularly school attendance. In 8 cases care proceedings were brought by the education department on grounds of non-school attendance but school problems were also a significant factor in 10 other cases. Of these 10 cases, 8 were taken to court by the social services department (5 on 'beyond control grounds', 2 on 'proper development' and 1 on 'moral danger' grounds). Two others involved police prosecutions for criminal offences. In all cases both the education welfare officer (EWO) and the social worker were involved in the decision to take proceedings and in some cases school personnel, police and medical

people were also concerned.

In the 8 cases in which the education department made the application for a care order, the cases had been referred to the social services who were either familiar with the case or made appropriate investigations. In 7 of the cases a case conference was subsequently held with the EWO attending. In 5 of the cases there were clearly other problems concerning the child and his family which in themselves might have lead to a consideration of a care order. In evidentiary terms however, these other factors were less severe or less well defined and it was decided that the case would be best taken to court on the 'educational grounds'. This decision was jointly agreed in 4 cases with the social services giving the education department full support in reports, etc. In one case the EWO was under some pressure from the social worker to take the case and subsequently agreed to do so.

In the remaining three cases the social worker was not in agreement with the EWO's wish to obtain a full care order. In one instance the social worker felt that there were no major problems other than non-school attendance and the child was better remaining at home. In two cases the social worker thought that a supervision order would suffice as the family problems were not severe and were likely to improve.

In some cases family difficulties or problems with the child's development are the central issue and non-school attendance is seen as a symptom of more general disturbance. These cases are normally handled by the social services. The initiating action may be taken by the education department and the EWO is normally involved in the decision about how to proceed. There seems to be no reluctance expressed by EWOs if the social services are prepared to apply for a care order themselves. This pattern was clear in 3 cases; two taken on the grounds of the psychological development of the child and one on 'moral danger'. In the 5 cases when the case was brought as 'beyond control' the fact that the child was not attending school was seen as part of an overall pattern of behaviour, including the parents' inability to control the child, the child's absconding and involvement in criminal activities. The EWO tended to play a secondary role in these cases, reporting the non-school attendance to the social worker as additional information.

Case Conferences

The procedural guidelines for NAI cases in the 5 authorities recommend that case conferences be held in any case thought to involve NAI or where there is a risk of injury to a child. Some state that a conference must be held for all new referrals; others that the area officer should call a conference if necessary. The guidelines also specify that a case conference can recommend that a child may be placed on, or removed from, the child abuse register. Some go so far as to say that this is the only body with authority to make such decisions. Area officers (or directors) are responsible for calling and chairing NAI conferences, and NSPCC special unit personnel and child care advisors may also be involved. In discussion these personnel showed an awareness of their responsibilities and conferences are normally held in NAI cases. In all 13 cases in which a child was injured a case conference was held. A conference was also

Table V Membership of Case Conferences

	Number of Case Conferences Where Each Group Represented by One or More People	
	Proper Development Grounds	*Other Care Proceedings*
Medical		
Paediatrician	13	—
GP	7	—
Nursing Officers	18	—
Medical Social Worker	6	—
Health Visitor	25	2
Psychiatrist or Psychologist	2	5
Social Services		
Member of management (including resource management)	9	4
Child Care Advisor	7	4
Area Officer/Director	16	6
Team Leader or Senior	24	11
Case Social Worker	27	14
Court Officer	—	3
Family Aid/Home Help	3	1
Residential Worker	7	8
Education Welfare Officers	2	11
Teacher/Headmistress	4	8
Housing Department	5	—
Probation Officer	14	2
Police	14	1
NSPCC	16	1
Local Authority Solicitor	16	3
Parent	3	1
Membership not recorded	4	5
Total conferences	36	22
Mean Number	9	6
Range	4 – 16	4 – 9

held in 12 of the other 17 cases brought under proper development grounds. In care proceedings under all other grounds or in criminal prosecutions there were conferences held in 16 of the 24 cases. In some cases more than one conference may be held: in 11 cases there was more than one case conference. In one of the NAI cases four conferences had been held and in another five had been held. NAI case conferences tend to be larger and drawn from a wider range of agencies. (In all 'proper development' case conferences the average attendance was 9; in all conferences involving children who were injured the average number was 11; and in the first conference involving children who were injured the average attendance was 12.) Table V shows that medical staff in particular are involved in NAI conferences. Area officers or team leaders

are also more likely to attend these conferences in addition to the case social worker. Probation officers, police, NSPCC, and the local authority solicitor are all more likely to attend these conferences. On the other hand school personnel, EWOs, residential workers, psychiatrists/psychologists are more likely to attend conferences in other types of cases.

It was also noticeable from the files that NAI case conferences are more carefully recorded than other conferences. Formal minutes or records are more likely to be included in the file, the membership of the conference is more likely to be recorded and the outcomes of the conference formally specified Authorities differ widely in the extent and manner of recording the content of the meeting. In some there is only a short summary paragraph, in others the information relevant to the case mentioned during discussion is seperated from a record of participants' views, and in others a nearly verbatim account is attempted.

Case conferences have clearly become a standard feature of NAI cases. When a child is injured they are always called and the police normally invited. An NAI conference is usually formally recorded and copy of the record kept on the file. However NAI conferences can involve a large number of people despite recommendations in at least one guidline to keep the conference membership below 10. In general, the more serious the case, the larger the case conference. Both from records and from conferences attended during the study, it is clear that while large conferences are efficient as a method of information exchange, they are often too large to function properly as decision-making bodies. For example, the balance of a meeting can be upset if one agency is over-represented as occurred in one case where 11 people attended a conference of whom 7 were police representatives. In another instance a chairman of a large meeting faced with considerable disagreement resorted to taking a majority vote. There also appears to be a good deal of uncertainty about the status of case conference recommendations. Although the guidelines normally emphasise that the conference is for information exchange they also state that any changes in recommendations for action made by the conference must be referred back. The case conference is usually seen as a body which recommends but does not decide. However, case conference decisions are often referred to in files and other records.

Disagreement and Indecision

Decisions on whether or not to take legal proceedings are not always taken with certainty or total agreement amongst the people concerned. In 23 of the 54 cases involving care proceedings or criminal prosecutions there was some element of indecision or disagreement. Uncertainty about the decision can occur in relation to any of the main elements in the decision: the need of the child which requires intervention; the ability of the authority to provide suitable resources; whether the situation will change or develop in significant ways or whether the case can be substantiated in court.

Uncertainty about the need to intervene was the most common form of indecision (12/23 cases) and this was particularly true for 'proper development' cases (11). For example, uncertainty existed about whether

bruising to a child was caused accidentally or not, who had caused the injury, whether only one child or all the children were at risk, whether the mother's incompetence at providing physical care placed the child at risk. In two cases when a place of safety order had been made on a child, the case conference held later decided that the uncertainty was so great that no further action should be taken. The child was returned home. In 4 of the 11 'proper development' cases there was clear disagreement between people and in 2 of them the disagreement was still apparent when the case came to court.

The resources available for the child were a source of uncertainty in 3 cases. (There are relatively few cases when resources are overtly discussed). All three involved cases when it was either the child's criminal or educational behaviour which was the major source of concern. In two 'education' cases there was disagreement between the social worker and the EWO over the type of order necessary to supply the appropriate resources for the child. In both cases the social worker felt that supervision at home would be adequate whereas the EWO wanted the child to be placed in a community home under a full care order. In the third case, a criminal prosecution, the police wanted the child removed from the community, whereas the social services were unable to provide accommodation from which the child could not abscond. In all these cases the social services were being pressured to recommend an order by another agency which the social services felt was inappropriate since the resources available would not meet the needs of the child. In the social work interviews it was cases of this type that social workers mentioned as being inappropriate for the court action.

Uncertainty about contingencies was the major element in the decision process in 5 cases. In 2 the health of the mother was in doubt. Three cases involved relatively new referrals of children beyond their parents' control and efforts were being made to work with the family to find an alternative to care proceedings.

Uncertainty about the case in legal terms was a feature of a number of cases. In 11 cases the adequacy of the evidence was of major concern and in another 10 cases of minor concern. This is not a major problem when the grounds for the action are relatively specific and clearcut as for example, when care orders have been made on siblings, or as a result of truancy or criminal offences. However in relation to the more diffuse grounds of 'proper development' and 'moral danger' there can be considerable doubt as to what might constitute adequate evidence. This occurred in 14 of the 21 cases when there was concern about evidence. In two of these cases difficulties about evidence led to the case being withdrawn. (In one the children had made allegation against the father which they subsequently withdrew. In the other the child had been taken into voluntary care and the 'proper development' grounds therefore did not exist at that time.)

This review of the uncertainties and disagreements in cases can only give a general picture of the kinds of problems which arise. A more detailed picture would only emerge from a close observation study of meetings, conferences, etc. Except where a clear difference of view is made explicit and backed up with arguments, many disagreements and differences are smoothed over or avoided, particularly in written records. Consensus rather than conflict is

emphasised both during case conferences and in the records of these conferences. This was clearly observed when conferences were attended and the records of these events subsequently obtained. In other cases where 'hints' and 'clues' of disagreement emerged from a close reading of the files people were reluctant to discuss the issues. In some cases we found that this reluctance concealed major disagreements which were not made explicit and which only emerged when case came to court. It should however be noted that these kinds of instances are rare and in the majority of situations the case for taking proceedings is overwhelming and there is no disagreement between those involved.

The period before the hearing

Time, Delays and Placement of Children

After the decision is made to take legal proceedings the case must be prepared for court, information collected and collated, parties notified, court dates obtained, reports requested and written, etc. These activities take time and sometimes a considerable amount of organisation.

The length of time which elapses from the decision being taken to proceed and the hearing of the case can range from a week to more than a year. Of cases involving care proceedings only three were settled within 28 days and in two of these the case did not come to court as the decision was reversed by a case conference and the child returned home. A group of 18 cases were heard after 28 days and before 56 days had elapsed. But in 31 cases the time taken was in excess of 56 days; eleven of these took longer than 4 months and 2 longer than 6 months. One case has still not been heard at the end of the study period after 14 months. Wardship cases take significantly longer to come to court. All 9 wardship cases in the sample took in excess of 4 months and 4 took a year or more before the matter was settled. To some extent these delays reflect the uncertainty and unpredictable nature of cases which are taken to the high court. In 5 of the 9 cases the principal reason for delay was waiting for a court welfare officer or the Official Solicitor to make a report on the case. In one instance after waiting for 7 months the local authority solicitor and the solicitors for the parents came to an agreed solution, later ratified by the court, in order to resolve the certainties about the placement of the children.

In opposed S.2 resolution cases or when an application is made to revoke a care order the matter is either settled relatively quickly if there is a clear cut case either way or may continue for 6 months or more while the situation is monitored or agreement between the parties is sought.

If a place of safety order is obtained on a child the case must come before the juvenile court at the end of the period unless the child is returned home. Apart from the 8 day place of safety orders obtained by the police, most will run for 28 days. Occasionally orders are made for shorter periods if the local authority or the magistrates think the case can or should be heard in court by that time. In some areas it is expected that, unless some very good reason exists, the full hearing will take place after the 28 days. This policy appears to

emanate from the clerk of the court but has been accepted by the social services areas working with that court as a proper practice. In nine cases the full hearing took place at the expiry of a place of safety order. However it is common for at least one interim care order to be obtained before a full hearing of the case. This was true in 32 of the cases. This practice is mainly confined to cases brought by the social services. In only 2 of the 13 education or criminal cases were interim orders obtained. In these circumstances the child is normally living at home or remanded on bail. In 16 of the cases more than one interim care order was obtained (6 cases had two interim orders, 3 had 3 orders, 4 had 4 orders, 1 had 5 and in 1 case more than 12 orders were made).

In each case we tried to establish the main reasons for delays and particularly where delays exceeded 56 days. In areas when the juvenile court sits infrequently or where there is considerable pressure on court time, it is perhaps not unreasonable that obtaining a suitable date might result in delays of up to 8 weeks. However delays in excess of that time need explanation.

Court scheduling is a problem throughout the legal system and can certainly create difficulties in juvenile courts. Care proceedings can take up a significant amount of the available time when a court sits, for example, only one day every two weeks. Finding time for the court to hear a longer case can be difficult. Some courts are prepared to convene on a special day for care proceedings or arrangements may be made for additional courts to sit on the same day. If the child is being prosecuted for a series of criminal offences, or offences committed with others, the scheduling of cases can also cause difficulty. In 6 cases delays in excess of 8 weeks primarily resulted from difficulties in obtaining court dates.

Cases may be adjourned or interim orders made in order to ensure that a child is represented. If a case comes to court and the child is not represented the magistrates may adjourn the case to allow this to be organised. If the solicitor in a case has not had time to prepare his case he may ask for the case to be adjourned. In some cases the solicitor may not be able to attend. This usually happens in courts where several courts are running simultaneously and the solicitor is involved in another court room. The lack of scheduling of cases beforehand makes this inevitable. There were 6 cases in which adjournments to arrange representation contributed to longer delays.

Difficulties in ensuring that all the participants in a hearing are present can also result in cases being put off for an additional 28 days. Parents sometimes do not turn up for hearings or are not available (for example, because a parent is in prison, in hospital etc.) and courts are often reluctant to hear a case unless the parents are present. Witnesses may also not be available. In a well organised case the availability of witnesses should be dealt with at an early stage but in at least two instances failure to check and arrange availability meant that a full hearing could not go ahead. In both cases this appeared to result from uncertainty between the social worker and the local authority solicitor as to who was responsible for making the arrangements. In 5 cases the failure of witnesses or parents to turn up to a hearing contributed to the overall delay in settling the case.

Some of the most lengthy delays occurred when the care proceedings were not heard because of concurrent criminal prosecutions of the parents. Juvenile

courts will not in general hear a case which depends on the evidence of a child having been injured by its parent if the question of the parent's guilt is to be determined by another court. If the parent pleads guilty and the matter is dealt with in the magistrates court, the case may be heard relatively quickly. But if the case is contested or it goes to the crown court then very considerable delays may occur. It is unfortunate that it is in those cases where there is real doubt about whether the parent did injure the child in which these long delays occur, since these are the cases most likely to be contested. Because of the possible risk the child will normally be separated from his parents for a considerable period. In 5 cases there were significant delays as a result of criminal prosecutions of the parents; in 3 cases there were delays of about 5 months and in one the delay was more than a year.

In a number of cases delays occur because of uncertainties about the case itself or the circumstances of the family. For example, if the case is particularly concerned with the psychological development of the child, time may be needed to make a thorough assessment of the child, involving a number of specialists. In complex family situations it may be thought necessary for more information to be collected about the dynamics of the family. These kinds of reasons contributed to delays in 5 cases. In 10 cases delays mainly arose because of the changing circumstances of the family and the need to monitor and assess these changes. For example, time may be needed to allow the recovery of a parent from a period of mental or physical ill health; there may be concern about whether a cohabitee suspected of violence towards a child will continue to live with the mother or not. In some instances the monitoring strategy is explicit and well understood. In others it is much less well-defined and seems to reflect a general uncertainty about what should be done. At worst there is a 'wait and see' attitude. If the child is at home while such uncertainties are resolved then this is not a reason for concern. If however, the child has been removed from home then the matter should probably be resolved as quickly as possible.

Finally, in 3 cases delays resulted from appropriate placements not being available. In all three the decision to apply for a care order was based on the assessment that the children should be placed in a particular environment. In each case the child was left at home until the placement became available and the court date was then obtained for a hearing.

During the time which elapses before a case comes to court the children involved may be removed from their parents and their future remain uncertain. In 38 of the 54 care proceedings cases the children were moved from home at the beginning of the period; in 20 cases to a community home or assessment centre, 12 to foster parents and 6 to hospital. Some were also moved during the period; in 19 cases the children were moved once and in 4 cases twice. At the end of the period 22 were placed in a community home or assessment centre, 19 were fostered and 13 were living with their parents or relations. In the wardship cases 6 were placed in community homes and 3 were at home. (The lack of foster placements in these cases is a result of the fact that most of the wardship cases came from the London authority in which foster parents were scarce.) The majority of children who were placed in community homes awaiting the outcome of proceedings were over 10 but in 5 cases the

children were under 5 and in 2 cases under 1 year.

Local Authority Solicitor

The local authority legal department was involved in some way in the vast majority of cases brought by the local authority. The department was not concerned with cases brought by the police, namely the criminal cases and one care proceedings involving children who had been left at a policeman's house. In another case when a child had been abandoned the police presented the case although technically the application had been made by the social services. In 4 of the 8 education cases the local authority solicitor was not involved in any way.

Although the solicitor is brought into nearly all local authority cases he is often not directly involved in the decision whether or not to take proceedings. In only a third of cases could we find any evidence that the solicitor was included in the early decision phase. It was more common for this to happen in cases of non-accidental injury. In several of the authorities' procedural guidelines on NAI cases the solicitor is specified as an appropriate person to invite to a case conference. As noted above the solicitor does often attend these conferences. In other cases the more common practice is for the solicitor to be notified after the decision to proceed is taken. In Authority 3 private solicitors may be briefed due to the shortage of manpower in the legal department; 5 of the 13 local authority cases were handled by private solicitors after initial consultations with the local authority solicitor. One of them was a wardship case in which the local authority briefed a firm of London solicitors to act as their agent.

In the 51 cases in which the local authority was the applicant (including all wardship cases when the local authority was making a case for the child to be placed or kept in their care) there was considerable variation in the extent of direct involvement of the solicitor. In 18 cases there appeared to have been no face-to-face contact between the solicitor and the social worker. Liaison seems to have been conducted by letters and telephone calls. These cases all occurred in the non-metropolitan counties (6 in each authority) where physical distance creates travelling problems. In the two metropolitan authorities the solicitor had direct contact with the social worker in all cases. Overall the solicitor met with the social worker in 28 cases, although he only visited the area office in 13 of these. He attended a case conference in 20 cases. When the parents are making an application to revoke a care order and the local authority is the respondent there appears to be little direct involvement of the solicitor.

As far as could be ascertained, the communications between social workers and the solicitor in the preparation phase of the case were mainly handled in a polite and businesslike way. In about a third of the cases the solicitors appeared to show real concern over the case and the relationship was supportive. This was particularly so where the contact was handled on a personal, face-to-face basis. In a few cases however there was evidence of tension and misunderstanding. Occasionally communication is so limited that there is no agreement about the nature of the case. In one instance, the solicitor (in this case a private solicitor) had not been informed that a child was

in voluntary care until the court hearing and had to withdraw the case advising that a S.2 resolution would be a more appropriate legal procedure to use. In another case, although the social worker had not included the solicitor in discussions about the specific arrangements he wished to achieve in a wardship case, he complained that the solicitor had not understood his instructions. In both cases the social workers had apparently not understood the legal significance of information which they failed to tell the solicitor. Similar difficulties seem to underlie misunderstandings which arise about the social worker's own evidence. Sometimes the solicitor and social worker may not have discussed the social worker's evidence sufficiently to have reached a shared understanding of what the social worker is able to say and should say. But discussions can sometimes be of little help because the social worker does not understand the 'hearsay' rules or that the solicitor cannot ask leading questions in examination-in-chief. On the other hand solicitors are not particularly skilled at explaining these conventions to non-lawyers. Real difficulties occurred in court in 6 cases during the examination of the social worker by the solicitor which appeared to result from poor communication during the preparation of the case.

In several cases difficulties arose about witnesses being called and attending court. Three cases had to be adjourned because of the failure to arrange for witnesses to be present. In each case there appeared to be no agreement about who was responsible for making the arrangements prior to the hearing and both the social worker and the solicitor thought that the other was doing it. This difficulty is not uncommon. But where communication is relatively frequent and without negative preconceptions the problem is normally identified and sorted out well before the court hearing.

Misunderstandings during the preparation of a case were observed and were reported to us more frequently in relation to cases in authority 2. There was clear evidence that the poor relationships between social workers and the legal department which were apparent from the interview material were being played out in relation to particular cases. Difficulties in the relationship were not confined to this authority but in other authorities sufficient goodwill existed for problems to be resolved. When comparatively minor failures of communication occurred in authority 2 these were perceived by social workers as intentional acts and further contributed to their poor estimation of the services they received. For example, on occasions the solicitor had contacted the area officer about a case instead of the social worker. This was treated as a major issue rather than as a matter which could be put right quite simply.

The poor state of relationships in one authority is not of itself of greater significance. Difficulties between departments can arise in any large and dispersed organisation and the factors contributing to such a situation are usually complex. What is important is whether the organisational mechanisms and role relationships are sufficiently well developed to withstand minor stress. The fact that the lack of sympathy between the two departments can affect the handling of cases suggests that the organisational mechanisms are not adequate and that improvements could be made in the mutual understanding of roles and procedures in this, and perhaps in other authorities as well.

Private Solicitors

In all but 7 cases a private solicitor was involved in the case at some stage (including 1 in which the case was not ultimately proceeded with). A solicitor was involved in all the wardship, opposed S.2, and revocation cases, usually representing the parents (16 of the 18 cases). The child was represented in only 6 of these cases. In contrast, in all but 8 of the care and criminal proceedings the child was represented. (Those cases in which the child was not represented were not distinguished in any obvious way, such as by grounds). Usually it is only the child who is represented although in 6 cases both the child and the parent were represented in court by a solicitor or barrister. (In one case the grandparents were represented). In an additional 4 cases the parents consulted a solicitor but were not represented at the court hearing.

In the two metropolitan authorities it was much less common for the child to be represented, particularly in the London authority. In the three non-metropolitan counties there is a well-established pattern of the child being represented. The exceptions were 3 cases which did not go to court, 2 wardship cases, and 1 case where the solicitor for the child did not turn up at two successive court hearings and the case was heard without him on the second occasion. The juvenile courts in these counties (with one particular exception) prefer to see the child represented in any case when a care order might be considered and will normally adjourn the case if the child is not represented. This attitude is widely shared by the social service departments in these areas and the social workers (or in one case the courts officer section) take an active part in obtaining representation for the child. For example in 19 care proceedings in the non-metropolitan counties the social worker was clearly involved in obtaining representation for the child whereas this was recorded as having happened in only 2 cases in the metropolitan authorities.

The practice of parents being represented also varies between authorities and Authority 2 was particularly notable for the comparative frequency with which both parents and children were represented. There is no obvious reason why this should be so. While the area served by the authority is relatively affluent, the parents who obtained representation in these cases were neither economically nor educationally different from parents in other cases. The juvenile courts in the area tend to treat parents sympathetically and no one makes objection to the parents being represented. There are solicitors in the area who specialise in juvenile court work and they are perhaps more prepared to do the occasional case without payment or using the green form scheme[1]. These two factors are probably sufficient to create a situation where representation of parents is accepted and even encouraged.

Contact between a solicitor and the social worker in the case is usually confined to telephone calls; meetings were recorded as having taken place in 7 cases and letters were on file in 5. In a few cases extensive correspondence and discussions take place but these cases are rare and seem to concern difficulties about placement or where there are several children. They are not normally concerned with detailed consideration of evidence or the merits of a case.

---

[1] The 'green form scheme' is a provision whereby the legal aid fund will cover very limited consultation of a solicitor.

Using the telephone is obviously a quick and easy way to obtain information. However it has the disadvantage that if misunderstandings occur it is a very restricted and unrecorded form of communication. It also means that decisions about what to say and how to respond must be made on the spot and without prior thought. If a social worker is uncertain about how he should relate to a solicitor, the telephone is probably the most difficult method by which to communicate, particularly when the person is not known. It would not be surprising if social workers appeared reluctant to give information in this way. Where contact is made personally between individuals communication about cases seems to be much easier.

Juvenile courts

Juvenile courts are specially constituted magistrates courts. As such, the responsibility for their construction and maintenance rests with the local authority and the magistrates courts committee. Since juvenile courts were first set up in 1908, the aim has been to provide a tribunal separate from the adult courts and there have been various attempts to radically change the ordinary courts system. However the venues and facilities have only improved here and there. In 1960 the Ingleby Committee were still critical of the standards of premises, particularly waiting rooms and other ancilliary accommodation. In 1961, a working party was set up to consider the accommodation needs of juvenile courts in the metropolitan stipendiary courts area and a number of purpose-built courts have since been constructed in inner London and some provincial cities. Despite the intention to provide such specially designed courts on a wider basis, there remains a great variety in the physical settings in which juvenile courts are held.

Statutory provisions or governmental advisory circulars provide little in the way of specification for the design and organisation of juvenile courts.

They indicate that:

1. juvenile courts should sit as often as necessary (S. 47(1) CYPA 1933);
2. juvenile courts should not sit in the same room as one used for other hearings unless separated by an hour before and after (S. 47(2) CYPA 1933 modified by S. 17(2) 1963 C.A.);
3. the people present in the court should be limited to members and officers of the court, parties to the case, their solicitors and counsel, witnesses and other persons directly concerned, bona fide representatives of newspapers and newsagencies and such other persons as the court specially authorises (as in 2 above);
4. children waiting for courts should not mix with adult defendants (unless jointly charged or a relative) (S. 31 1933 CYPA);
5. a waiting room should be provided for children who are not in custody and their parents, children who are in care or in custody and their escorts and a secure room for unruly children. The first two can be combined, but should be ordinary rooms, preferably with windows and ordinary furniture conveniently located to the court (recommendation of Home Office circular 39/1971);

6. some accommodation should be provided for officers of the local authority attending the court. (Home Office circular op. cit.)

Juvenile courts are located in three main types of building. The juvenile court may be one of a number housed in a court complex. These complexes of crown, county and magistrates courts with ancilliary officers for justices' clerks, probation officers, etc. are usually modern and self contained. Some are part of a larger complex of municipal buildings and may be adjacent to a major police station. They are normally found in the larger provincial cities where the volume of cases has justified building facilities of this kind. Secondly in smaller towns the court may also be located in a separate courthouse. These are usually smaller and older premises, containing only one or two magistrates courts and a few offices. They are often next to a police station. Thirdly, the court may be located in a building serving more general purposes. Municipal department buildings are commonly used in this way. The buildings and often the courtrooms are not primarily 'legal' in character and the rooms may be only temporarily used as courts.

It is rare for the waiting facilities available for the juvenile court to conform to the recommendations of the Home Office circular. Most commonly the waiting area is confined to the corridors or foyers outside the courtrooms. If several courts are sitting or if there is a long list of juvenile criminal cases these areas may become extremely crowded, noisy and confused. In modern courts more extensive provision for waiting may be made. In the smaller, older courts where only a few cases are to be heard a small foyer may be adequate. The waiting area for the court is of much greater significance to parents, children and witnesses than it is to the court personnel. It is the first point of contact with the court and considerably more time may be spent waiting for a case to be called than during the actual court hearing. The waiting area may be much more significant in creating an impression of the court than what happens in the courtroom. The waiting period is often important for the professionals in the case as this may be the only occasion on which they all meet. It provides an opportunity to clarify points of the case, exchange information and correct any misunderstandings. Personal contact can be made and relationships developed and the physical character of the waiting area can facilitate or hinder these interactions.

The rooms used as courtrooms for juvenile cases vary considerably both in size and style. In some cases extremely formal, large and impressive magistrates courts are used. The court contains traditional fitted furniture and the magistrates are raised to some height above the rest of the court. These rooms usually only have windows in the ceiling and are shut-off and enclosed. Even modern magistrates courts preserve this general character, although the furniture may be more modern and the physical separation of participants less extreme.

Purpose-built juvenile courts are usually medium to small in size and are light and airy without the claustrophobic feeling of the traditional courts. The room is more informal in appearance. Tables and chairs replace the old-fashioned boxed furniture, and the legal trappings of dock and witness box are usually absent. Some formal features do remain, for example, the raised magistrates' bench and nominal witness boxes, and the design therefore tends

to retain its legal character. In a few courthouses these courtrooms are self-contained with their own waiting facilities and interview rooms and a separate entrance.

Some juvenile courtrooms have clearly been converted from other uses and do not have the full legal trappings of a formal courtroom. They often look not unlike committee rooms, school rooms or village halls. As such they must appear more familiar to many of the participants. In some cases they are rooms which are still used for other purposes, for example a council chamber, a library or a meeting room.

Juvenile courts are individually organised and whether a sitting proceeds smoothly or becomes chaotic depends to a large extent on how the court personnel organise the cases to be heard. Depending on their relationship with the court, social service departments, individual social workers and solicitors may be able to influence general court organisation, as well as the hearing of individual cases. Court information systems are notoriously archaic although in some areas computerised lists of cases are now in use. These greatly assist in arranging court lists and keeping records of adjournments, outcomes, etc.

Courts vary in their practices regarding scheduling of care proceedings. Some achieve the separation of care cases and criminal cases by holding hearings at different times. In others the volume of cases is either too small or too large to make this possible. Where care and criminal cases are heard on the same day some courts give care cases priority over criminal cases. This practice both minimizes the mixing of those involved in care cases with others and reduces the time spent waiting for care cases to be heard. In other courts care proceedings are given no priority, merely being called as part of a court list. Some courts go to the extreme of only calling care cases after the criminal proceedings have been dealt with. Care proceedings can take a long time and it is thought better to hear the shorter cases first. This allows a greater number of people to be released.

During this study we came to the conclusion from observation that the physical character of juvenile courts is of considerable importance. The physical setting and courtroom design of juvenile courts play an important part in setting the social character of court hearings. They give cues to participants about the seriousness and authority of the proceedings. The type of furniture used and its positioning indicates the differing roles and statuses of those involved. They also constrain the range of activities in which a person may engage and the roles he may play. Physical discomfort may also distract participants or increase the unpleasantness of the experience. These considerations all affect both the professionals involved and the parents and children directly concerned in the case.

During the course of the study, proceedings were observed in many different juvenile court settings. Each court had its own physical and social character. Since few people other than lawyers have the opportunity to visit a number of courts and so little is published on the character of courts, we have included a brief description of the main juvenile courts serving the areas included in the study.

Local Authority 1. All juvenile cases from this local authority are dealt with by

one juvenile court which serves and is located in an adjoining borough. The court is difficult to get to; it is some distance from the main centre of the authority area and is not well-placed for public transport. The juvenile court is situated within a court complex. Police cells are located in the basement, the ground floor is predominantly taken up by the courtrooms with administrative offices occupying the first floor. There are no special waiting room facilities, the waiting area being restricted to an entrance hall and corridors. Nor are there facilities for speaking privately. There is no enquiry desk and no clearly displayed notices. The usher calls the case names and location. The waiting area is usually extremely crowded and confused. At the beginning of a session there may be fifty or more people waiting, yet the only place to sit is on narrow wooden forms lining one side of the corridors. The only refreshment facilities available are in the basement, but access is mainly restricted to the police. There appears to be only one toilet and one public telephone is provided.

There are five courtrooms in all, and care proceedings took place in three. Most cases were heard in a large old-fashioned magistrates court where an impressive coat-of-arms hangs behind the magistrates' raised bench. Because of the room's high ceilings and size it is often difficult to hear what is being said. This room also provides the sole access to cells below and constant traffic tends to disrupt proceedings. The second court room is designated as the juvenile courtroom. It is light, airy and less formal. The furniture consists of tables and chairs rather than purpose-built boxes and although fairly large, only half the room is generally used. The third room appears to have been a magistrates' retiring room. It is relatively small and, because of overlarge furniture, becomes crowded and difficult to move around in.

The juvenile court meets for one morning each week and all five courts may be used. There is no scheduling of cases and all participants must attend at 10.00 a.m. Care proceedings are mixed with criminal cases and given no priority, merely being called as part of a list which continually changes. It is impossible to tell when cases will be heard and people have to wait outside the court door. Those who are appearing in more than one case have difficulty timetabling their appearances, although this can be facilitated by friendships with court staff.

Local Authority 2. (a) The juvenile court in the seaside town is situated on the lower ground level of a purpose-built modern court house near the centre of the town and next to the public library. The courthouse is not connected to a police station and the juvenile court has a separate entrance. Participants wait in the narrow corridor outside the court-room. There is also a small waiting room which is used for consultation. Cases we observed were called straight in and the waiting area was not under stress. Another room in the building is sometimes used as an auxiliary court. The waiting facilities here are good with two rooms available both containing tables and chairs. The designated juvenile courtroom is modern and purpose-built. It has a raised bench and preserves the formal court layout. However the furniture is bright and modern. The auxiliary courtroom is a small, pleasant room, with pale wood furniture, carpeted floors and external windows. Although the magistrates are slightly raised at one end all participants sit around a large table. Care proceedings are

heard separately from criminal cases. Interim care orders are generally dealt with first, followed by more lengthy proceedings. Scheduling of cases does not appear to be a problem.

(b) The courthouse used by the area on the fringe of London is situated in a 12 year old complex of public buildings in the town centre. A waiting room is located on the same floor as the juvenile courtroom. It is not within the earshot of the courtroom and people tend to wait in the narrow corridor outside the courtroom where there is no seating. There are toilets, public telephones and a clearly indicated enquiries desk. Refreshments are available from a coffee machine in an upstairs lounge (when it is working). The lounge contains three small partitioned sections where private conversations can be held. As with the waiting room, these facilities are only used if someone, a social worker, a solicitor or clerk, is prepared to inform people when the case is ready to be heard. One courtroom is used for juvenile cases and this is some distance from the other courts. The courtroom is large, light, and airy, the bench is slightly raised and everyone sits at tables and chairs. A nominal witness stand is placed by the bench.

Parents and children are generally seated alone in the middle of the large room and appear very vulnerable. It is also awkward for solicitors to get instructions during a case as this involves walking across the open space. The juvenile court meets on one morning per week, although extra sessions are arranged if necessary. Cases are not scheduled and care proceedings are given no special priority.

(c) The juvenile court serving the town and surrounding rural area is held in the magistrates courts adjoining the local police station. It is a small red brick building close to the railway station convenient for the social workers who are housed nearby but is some distance from the town centre. A small foyer outside the juvenile courtroom and an anteroom through the adult court are available for waiting. Seating and waiting space is adequate for the small numbers of people involved. There are separate facilities for solicitors to interview their clients. There are two courtrooms; one is traditional magistrates court and the other is designated as a juvenile courtroom. The latter is small and furnished with tables and chairs. It is inclined to get over-crowded and is awkward to move around in. The juvenile court sits once every three weeks and there appears to be good scheduling of cases. Although no priority is given to care proceedings, social workers seem to be able to ensure that there are not unnecessary delays.

Local Authority 3. (a) Two of the areas included in the study use the court facilities in the main county town. The courts are located close to the town centre in a large complex of buildings. These primarily house municipal offices and give the impression of a guildhall rather than a court. Occasionally an old library room located in another public building some distance away is used. The waiting area for the main courts is restricted to the passage giving access to the courtrooms. It is totally inadequate for the long lists of cases that are generally scheduled. The seating is sparse and uncomfortable and the area is typically packed to capacity. There are no refreshment facilities, interview rooms, public telephones or enquiries desk. The toilet facilities are hard to

find. The area is in need of decoration and the general atmosphere is one of decay and gloom. For the auxiliary courtroom the stairs offer the only available waiting area.

Of the two main courtrooms, only one appears to be used for care proceedings. This room is large, light and airy, and in appearance resembles a school room. Witnesses, after giving evidence, are seated on a raised platform at one end, while the magistrates' bench is similarly slightly raised at the other end. The room is dominated by a large table in the centre, around which are seated the clerk, solicitors, parents and children. The old library room is very small and surrounded by empty book shelves with two tables and a bench. The juvenile court sits once a week. Care proceedings are given high priority and special sittings can be arranged. In general, however, care and criminal cases are heard on the same day.

(b) There are courts in two towns in this geographically large area. However, care cases are usually heard in the court in the seaside town reflecting problems which arise with a holiday population. The juvenile court is contained in a building which also houses the police station and some administrative offices. Since people may have to travel some distance to attend this court its location opposite the railway station is convenient. The foyer of the principal courtroom with seating for about six is used for waiting, providing ample room for the numbers typically expected. A corridor lined with benches is used when an additional room serves as a court. An interview room is provided and toilet facilities are available, but no refreshments can be obtained. The courtroom is a large, bright and airy room. With its informal layout and stripped pine furniture, it resembles a school room rather than a law court. There are two witness boxes, no more than moveable wooden railings, and the magistrates are only slightly raised on a wooden platform. Very occasionally a small room which might be a magistrates' retiring room is used. The juvenile court meets one day a month usually with only a couple of cases to be heard. Criminal and care cases are mixed and care proceedings are not given priority. However social workers or solicitors do seem able to arrange the timetabling of cases with the clerk.

(c) The court in this industrial and seaside town is situated on the first floor of the Victorian town hall. The building is in the town centre and is mostly taken up by municipal offices. The waiting area is inadequate for the numbers of people involved in cases. There is only a landing and hallway outside the courtroom with a few benches along the wall. There are no interview rooms, nor convenient places for a private conversation. No refreshments are available, smoking is not permitted and the only toilets are difficult to find and some distance away from the waiting area. Juvenile cases are heard in either the regular magistrates court or the council chamber. Care proceedings are usually heard in the council chamber which is a large room with semicircular banks of seats and a curved dias, all in lavishly carved wood. An overhanging public gallery adds to the impressive appearance. The magistrates' courtroom is classic in design. With its dark-wood and old-fashioned furniture, large dock and raised bench, it is an awe-inspiring setting for youngsters and those unfamiliar with courts of law. The juvenile court is held fortnightly, but with approximately 25 cases listed per session this may be altered to weekly sittings.

Care and criminal proceedings are heard on the same day but care proceedings seem to be given priority being heard first and in a separate courtroom.

Local Authority 4. (a) The court complex in the county town includes adult and juvenile courts, various court offices and retiring rooms and is located on the second floor of the Police Headquarters building. Signs indicating the existence of courtrooms in the building are small and insignificant compared to the bold, gold lettering which marks the entrance to the police station. It is situated on a busy arterial road within walking distance of both the bus station and the town centre. There is no waiting room provided and people wait in the narrow corridor outside the juvenile courtrooms. The large concourse outside the adult courtrooms is rarely used as it is not in earshot of the courts. Although the corridor contains numerous chairs, the seating is totally inadequate on days when criminal cases are heard. The situation is somewhat better when care proceedings are heard as fewer people are involved. There are no rooms for consultation. Toilets, public telephones and a coffee machine are some distance away from the juvenile courtrooms. The coffee machine works only intermittently. The police canteen in the basement is used by solicitors and social workers but not usually by parents or witnesses. Three rooms are used for the hearing of juvenile cases; two are designated juvenile courtrooms. One resembles a traditional courtroom with a dock and witness box although the magistrates do not sit on a raised platform. Windows with an external view along one wall produce a light atmosphere. The room is fairly small and cluttered, making it difficult for people to move around. A storage room is located at the rear and persistent traffic to it can be distracting. The second courtroom is less formal in its design. The justices' library is also used as an auxiliary courtroom if the need arises.

At the start of the study period the juvenile court met once a week. Cases were not scheduled, all participants being expected to turn up for the start of the session. The timetabling of cases appeared chaotic, with care cases being accorded no priority. During the study, however, it was decided that care proceedings should be held at a separate afternoon sitting. Too many cases were being set down for each session and the volume of care proceedings justified a specified time. This separation resulted in a far more relaxed waiting atmosphere. Attempts were made to timetable cases for the convenience of the participants and both social workers and solicitors arranged times with the clerk.

(b) In the small country town serving a rural area the court complex and police station are located within the same modern, purpose-built building. The two courtrooms, their waiting rooms and administrative offices have a separate entrance. Outside the building there is a 'portacabin' which is used almost exclusively as a domestic court. There are considerable transport difficulties to this court as the town is not served by a railway station and the court is located on the outskirts of the town. Each courtroom has one small waiting room. These are pleasant, light rooms and fairly intimate in design. Leather-padded couches run along the walls with low coffee tables in front. Seating is adequate and the rooms only become crowded when a domestic court is sitting at the same time. Telephones are available in the offices but not

in the public area and toilet facilities are provided. There are no consulting rooms. Two courtrooms are available for juvenile proceedings, but despite the building being of recent design, neither is a purpose-built juvenile courtroom. The room used for adult cases doubles as the juvenile court. In appearance the courtroom is very 'businesslike' with modern furniture which is smart as well as functional. It is moveable and can be rearranged. The room resembles a committee room more than a court. The second courtroom is only occasionally used for juvenile cases. It is larger, formal in design and more imposing than the other courtroom. The juvenile court meets fortnightly with usually only one bench being necessary. Cases are scheduled, with the list being prepared by the clerk. The courts officer and probation liaise with him to order the cases in the most convenient way. Care proceedings are usually heard after the other cases have been dealt with, although they may be heard in a separate court when the list is long.

(c) The well-established country town uses a small, old-fashioned courthouse built in 1916. It is typical of those found in provincial towns where the volume of cases has not increased sufficiently to warrant the building of a new complex. Compared to the modern police station adjoining it, the court building has a very run-down appearance. It is located some minutes walk away from the town centre. The waiting facilities are inadequate and unsuitable. The front door of the courthouse opens into a waiting foyer. Apart from a couple of small wooden benches, there are only 17 chairs in all, some of which are unuseable. People tend to sit on a large table in the centre of the foyer, or in a side room cluttered with spare furniture. An empty room marked 'lady witnesses waiting room' could accommodate an overflow, but remains unused. The foyer is not clean, with cigarette butts scattered on the dirty floor. The walls and doors are covered with ancient grime. To add to the general impression of gloom, the lighting is very dim. There are toilets but as these are down an unlit, unmarked corridor they are not easily located by a newcomer. There are no refreshment facilities in the public waiting area, nor in the vicinity of the courthouse. The solicitors have their own room, with a telephone, but other participants are not given access to it and there are no rooms available for private conversations. Through a doorway at one end of the foyer are two courtrooms. The atmosphere here is in marked contrast to that of the foyer, the area being bright and freshly decorated. Both rooms are traditional in design. The larger of the two, used for the hearing of criminal cases, is more formal and dominated by a large dock. The second is smaller and slightly more informal in setting and is preferred for care proceedings. It is however very cramped, with narrow passageways making movement difficult. Solicitors have to half-turn to make contact with their clients, and social service representatives are often hidden behind the solicitors. The juvenile court sits once a week, hearing both criminal and care proceedings. Both courtrooms may be used if necessary. Cases are not scheduled, with all participants being required to turn up for the start of the morning session. The clerk tries to get care cases heard first in the smaller courtroom.

Local Authority 5. (a) The juvenile court in the centre of town which is used by three area offices is part of a whole court complex. It is situated only about

five minutes walk from the town centre. The building is large, modern, and was purpose-built only a few years ago. Separation of the different types of courts is a feature of the complex. The juvenile court on the ground floor and the adult courts upstairs are designed as self-contained units with their own waiting and interview facilities. The waiting facilities of the juvenile unit include a waiting room for parents and children, cells, a separate room for children remanded into care, and several interview rooms. Adequate seating is provided. There is a separate side entrance but this is rarely used, participants preferring to use the main entrance. An enquiries desk is placed close to the entrance and a noticeboard is well-positioned giving the location of cases listed for the day. Public telephones are provided. Separate toilet facilities for men and women are provided close to the waiting room. Refreshments are available from a machine located in one of the adult waiting rooms upstairs. The waiting facilities in these courts were the only ones we observed which really comply with the recommendations of the Home Office guidelines. There is only one courtroom in the juvenile unit. When a case is expected to take a considerable time, the domestic court upstairs is used. The juvenile courtroom was purpose-built and contains many modern features, including air-conditioning and a microphone system which can be used both to call cases and to amplify voices in the courtroom. The room is fairly compact with little distance between participants. There is no witness box or dock, and solicitors, children and parents all sit round a large table. A note of formality is however introduced by the magistrates' platform being raised several steps from the floor-level and the royal coat-of-arms hanging on the wall behind. The juvenile court sits twice weekly and lists often take up a whole day. There is no scheduling of cases, everyone being expected to turn up at 10.15 a.m. Care proceedings were generally heard after criminal cases but the court officer can influence the day's timetabling.

(b) The magistrates court complex in another town in the authority is new and modern in design. It houses courtrooms, administrative offices and the probation and after care service. The police station is adjacent. The complex is a few minutes walk from the town centre. A large area, lined with padded benches outside each of the courtrooms, is used for waiting. Despite considerable space and seating the facilities can become overstretched.

No special interview rooms seemed to be available and there are no public refreshment facilities. Toilet facilities and a public telephone are provided. There is an enquiries desk but this was unmanned on the occasions we visited. Two courtrooms are used for juvenile cases. If the list is fairly full then one is used for care proceedings, the other for criminal. The large courtroom used for care cases is a modern version of the classic style with all the legal trappings. The bench in juvenile proceedings does not sit on high, preferring to use a platform which is only very slightly raised. However the raised dias is still a dominant and impressive feature in the room. Because of the large size of the room and its high ceilings, voices tend to become lost and parents and children may have difficulty in hearing as they are seated behind the advocate's desk. There are no windows and the room has an enclosed atmosphere. The juvenile court sits fortnightly, hearing both care and criminal cases. Cases seem not to be scheduled, but social workers and solicitors can influence the clerk's

timetabling.

(c) The third court in the authority is part of a complex containing other municipal offices and is situated in the centre of a town. The main space used for waiting is a curved staircase with small landings. There is no seating and the area tends to become cramped. There is a waiting room situated on the same level as the courtroom and on the floor below there are a number of interview rooms and rooms for advocates. These are not within easy call of the courtroom and participants tend not to use them. There are no refreshment facilities. Toilets are provided close to the courtroom. There is only one courtroom and this is large, light and airy. Apart from a slightly raised magistrates' bench it does not look like a courtroom. The room is long and oblong in shape. Parents and children are seated towards the rear of the room and there is some distance between the various participants. This court is administered by the same clerk as the previous court and sits fortnightly, alternating with the other court.

In summary, in many courts the poor conditions provided for waiting areas which were criticised by the Ingelby Committee are still far from satisfactory today. In those courts which hear very few cases the foyers, lobbies and corridors normally used do not create problems for those few people who use them for short periods. When care cases are called straight into court the waiting area is of less importance except that a crowded waiting area can still be confusing and worrying for participants, both lay and professional. Even in some of the newly built courts the amount of waiting space, seating and facilities for private conversation are insufficient. In a number of courts relatively simple changes could significantly improve the waiting areas. Greater attention to decor and cleanliness, the provision of large and clear notices, better communication systems for announcing when cases are ready to begin and the provision of minimal refreshments could all make a considerable difference to the experience of those attending the court. (These comments on the waiting areas around juvenile courts are based on observations made by the research team. Morris and Giller (1977) also concluded that the waiting areas were unsatisfactory after interviewing both parents and children involved in criminal trials.)

It is still fairly common for care cases and criminal cases to be heard on the same day and people involved in the two types of cases to mix in the waiting area. This is unfortunate and certainly contributes to the parents' feeling that a care order is a form of punishment for them. Where care cases are heard on a separate day the situation is much improved. The more relaxed atmosphere greatly improves the chances for matters to be discussed between the participants before going to court. The pressure on courts or the unavailability of magistrates may make this arrangement impossible in some places. When the mixing of cases is inevitable either the specific time scheduling of care cases to avoid waiting or the provision of a separate room for people involved in care cases to wait would at least lessen the worst aspects. Long waiting times are undesirable in any circumstances particularly when a child is present. It is extremely wasteful of professionals' time and in some instances means that witnesses are not prepared to take part.

The continued use of large old-fashioned magistrates courts for care cases is

regrettable. These courts are extremely formal and imposing. It is often difficult to hear what is being said and there is sometimes extraneous comings and goings of people not directly concerned in the case. Parents and children have sufficient problems in understanding the proceedings without additional difficulties being created by the physical environment.

Juvenile court hearings

In the following discussion of proceedings in the juvenile court, full information on the hearings was obtained in 33 cases which were observed by members of the research team. More limited information on 16 additional hearings which were not observed was obtained from people who had been present. This information is restricted to factual matters such as the number of witnesses, who was represented, whether a report was submitted and the outcome. Detailed observation of such matters as timing and procedure and evaluations of the performance of the participants could only be made by an observer present at the time.

People Present At Hearings. Despite the recommendation that the people in court during care proceedings should be restricted, there are usually quite a number present. In a typical hearing there are three magistrates on the bench, a clerk, the parents and child, the local authority solicitor, the child's solicitor, a courts officer or senior social worker, an usher or sergeant and perhaps three witnesses who remain after giving evidence. In the cases we observed the average number in court was 14 and ranged from 10 to a maximum of 22.

The local authority solicitor usually presents the local authority's case. In the sample of cases this included cases brought under the education ground with the exception of two which were presented by an education welfare officer. Prosecuting solicitors presented the case when the police were bringing criminal prosecutions and in one the local authority solicitor mainly responsible for care cases was involved. In some a back-up solicitor from the department appeared (3) or a private solicitor briefed by the legal department (2). (Four of these five cases were due to the manpower problems in Authority 3). In 35 of the 49 cases which were fully heard in court, the child was represented and in 6 both the parents and child were represented. The representation was usually by a solicitor, only 7 involving a barrister. Briefing counsel occurred in the London authority either because the case was handled by a clerk who had no right of audience or for economic reasons. In Authority 2 barristers were briefed in 3 strongly contested cases. This is part of the pattern of more active representation in this county. In the other three authorities a solicitor briefed a barrister in only one case because he was on holiday when the case came to court.

The child was present in court in all observed cases when he or she was over 5 years of age, except in one case when the child was ill. In a few cases a child under 5 was brought to the court and shown to the magistrates and then taken away. A member of the child's family was also present in all observed cases except one. In this case the mother was mentally disturbed and there had been four interim orders made in respect of the child to that date. The magistrates were very concerned at the absence of the mother. After waiting for a short

period they finally agreed to hear the case to resolve the uncertainty surrounding a child's placement. In 18 cases both the mother and father were present; one parent present in the remainder.

In virtually all cases brought by the local authority a social worker from the social services is called as a witness unless no witnesses are called at all. Usually it is the current social worker in the case. In cases not previously known to the department a duty officer, senior social worker or team leader may give evidence instead. It is unusual for a social worker to be a witness in education or criminal cases (2 out of 13). In many cases another member of the social services department is also present at court. In cases which we observed the courts officer was in court in 16 and a senior social worker or team leader in 11. There were only 6 cases where no one other than the social worker attended court. The practice follows the pattern in the courts officer role described in the previous chapter: in Authorities 1, 4 and 5 where the role is more developed it was more usual for a courts officer to be present whereas a team leader was more frequently present in the other authorities. The presence of a member of the department to see the whole of the case and to give support to the social worker is thus a common feature of care proceedings. In contrast it was comparatively rare for other social workers to be present as observers (6 observed cases). The potential training opportunity provided by observing a case does not appear to be widely used in practice.

Time Waiting for Hearings. Participants are required to be present at the courthouse at a specified time. In the cases we observed some were called to court immediately but in others people waited up to 2½ hours for the hearing to begin. The average time spent waiting was 45 minutes although half the cases were called in less than ½ an hour. All the cases heard in the court serving the London Authority had to wait for a considerable period and the waiting conditions in this court are particularly poor. The other instances in which there were long delays occurred in courts where both criminal and care cases were being heard and when no priority was given to care cases. In a third of the cases the time spent waiting was longer than the time spent hearing the case.

The Hearing of the Facts. The CYPA 1969 clearly specifies that the applicant must prove a case under one of the specified grounds before the court considers the appropriate means of disposing of the case. In criminal proceedings it must also be established whether the child is guilty or not guilty of the offence. In 4 of the 44 care proceedings which were heard and were included in the sample no witnesses were called as to the facts of the case and the local authority solicitor (or EWO) briefly summarised the facts in opening the case. In one instance the child had been abandoned and the parents were not available. In another the mother was present and said she agreed with the facts as outlined. In neither of these cases was the child or the parents represented. In a third case the facts of the child's non-school attendance were given by the EWO presenting the case, in a sense acting as both witness and applicant. In a fourth case witnesses were available but were not called as the representatives of both the parent and the child said that they had read the

social enquiry report and were recommending a care order. The report and a written letter from a doctor were taken as evidence. In 4 of the 5 criminal cases in the sample the child pleaded guilty to the offence and no evidence was heard.

When witnesses are called by the applicant the most common number to be called is three (15 cases). In eight cases 1 witness was called and in another eight 2 were called. Sometimes a larger number of witnesses are called and in three cases there were as many as 7 witnesses. Large numbers tend to be involved when the grounds are proper development (a or b) although this is not always so. As mentioned above, the social worker is nearly always called. Other witnesses include medical personnel (12 cases), police (13 cases), EWO (9 cases), psychiatrists or psychologists (6 cases), probation officers (3 cases) and occasionally the parent or relative may be called by the local authority.

Witnesses were called by either the parent or the child in 19 of the 49 cases which were heard. In no cases did both the parent and child call witnesses. In 9 cases witnesses were called by the solicitor representing the child and these were usually the mother (6), the father (4) or the child (3). In only 2 cases were professional people called as witnesses; in one the social worker was called by the child and in another a residential social worker was called. The same pattern is true for the parents; the mother was a witness in 9 cases, the father in 4, other relatives or friends in 3 and in one case a nursing officer. In half these cases the witnesses were called by the solicitor representing the parents and in the other half by the parents themselves. In 21 cases where the child was represented (including one when both the child and parent were represented) no witnesses were called either by the child or the parent.

In relation to the discussion of the role of the representative of the child, these figures show that in three-quarters of the cases the solicitor confined himself to responding to information presented by witnesses called by other parties and in half the cases the witnesses were all called by the local authority. In addition, the witnesses called for the child or the parent were nearly always the parents. There can of course be some co-operation between all the solicitors in the matter of who calls which witness. Clearly the child's solicitor is prepared to leave it to the parents to appear as witnesses on their own behalf if they wish to do so. In the matter of professional witnesses it may be agreed beforehand that the local authority should call these witnesses, perhaps even those suggested by the child's solicitor. In the absence of a representative for the child the local authority may themselves call the parents.

Other than calling witnesses to give evidence on the facts of the case, documentary evidence is sometimes available. This is normally confined to school attendance records which are always submitted in education cases and medical evidence which is sometimes submitted when the appropriate doctor is not available to give evidence. This occurred in 10 cases. Documentary evidence is also provided in relation to criminal convictions relevant to the case (for example when the grounds are 'same household') or orders made by another court in respect of the child (for example, a supervision order). In the main however the evidence in care proceedings is taken orally from witnesses.

The wording of the CYPA 1969 suggests that in proving the case evidence should be adduced both in relation to the specific grounds of the application

and the general ground that the child is in need of care and control which it would not otherwise receive. In the cases which we observed these two 'legs' to proving the case were mentioned in 6 cases but in only 3 was a real distinction made in evidence. It is, of course, often difficult to separate the evidence which goes to prove the two legs, particularly in relation to the 'proper development' and 'in moral danger' grounds. One witness, particularly a social worker, may give evidence in relation to both. However it was presumably the intention of the Act that some explicit consideration should be given to both aspects of the case.

There is considerable variation in the length of time taken to hear the evidence in relation to proving the case, ranging from only a few minutes to 6 hours. The average time taken is 1½ hours but half the cases were heard in less than one hour. The length of time taken to hear the facts in the case is largely a function of the number of witnesses called. Representation of a child or both the children and the parents does not of itself contribute to lengthening hearings since, as was noted above, solicitors representing a child do not always call witnesses and parents may call witnesses even when they are not represented. The number of witnesses called and the time taken by hearing the evidence are both determined by whether the case is opposed or not. Witnesses are likely to be called by the child or the parents when the case is opposed; in 11 out of the 13 observed cases which were opposed and only 4 out of the 20 observed cases which were unopposed. The local authority is also likely to call more witnesses when they know there is opposition to the case (an average of 4 witnesses in opposed cases and 2 in unopposed).

At the conclusion of the presentation of the case the magistrates may retire to consider whether the case has been proved and they did so in a third of the observed cases. They may however only have a brief word amongst themselves. Of all the cases heard in the juvenile court there were only 2 when the case was found not to have been proved. One case involved care proceedings brought by the Police and the social worker had been opposed to the proceedings being brought. (This case involved a gypsy family who were being harassed by neighbourhood people. The father left his children at the police house as a protest against the police taking no action to stop the harassment). In a second case the social services had wanted a care order but the magistrates found the facts insufficient. The solicitor representing the child had argued for a care order but the parent's solicitor had strongly argued that on the evidence presented, there was no case.

The Disposition of the Case. Of the 47 cases where the court considered the disposition of the case, a social enquiry report was submitted in 44. The social worker who wrote the report was present in court to speak to it in 38 cases. The social enquiry report is extremely important both in the preparation of the case and in the part it plays in court hearings. A detailed discussion of these reports is included at the end of this section on court hearings.

In all but 5 cases the social worker recommended that a care order should be made. A supervision order was recommended in 3 of the education cases (see discussion above about disagreements between social workers and EWO's). A supervision order was also recommended in 2 'proper development' cases

involving suspected non-accidental injury to a child. When we made enquiries as to why this recommendation was made it appeared that in both cases there was some doubt about whether the evidence was sufficiently strong and that asking for a supervision order recognised the element of doubt. In one case recommending a supervision rather than a care order had been suggested by the local authority solicitor. While this strategy may be realistic in terms of obtaining an appropriate order in cases where non-accidental injury is suspected but not proved, it involves a confusion of the need to prove the case with the question of the proper disposal of it.

When a solicitor represents a child in care proceedings it does not follow that he will oppose the recommendations made by the local authority. In 12 cases he did oppose the recommendation but in 18 cases he supported the recommendation and in 8 remained neutral. The parents too may support the local authority's recommendation and did so in 13 cases, principally in those cases when they themselves admitted their inability to control the child (case brought under 'beyond control', 'education' and criminal cases). However the parents were opposed to the recommendation in 20 cases.

Although the court has no power to determine how the local authority will exercise its powers in relation to a care order, the arangements that may be made for a child are sometimes raised in court. The parents or the child's solicitor may try to extract promises from the social services in relation to such matters as the likelihood of the child being returned home, access to the child by the parents and the placement of the child. The magistrates may also express their views on these matters. In 12 cases the social worker gave undertakings on matters relating to the future of the child. In some instances the social services regard the views expressed by the magistrates as having the force of the law, or at least as a view that they should respect. This is particularly the case in areas where regular meetings are held with magistrates and information is given on the subsequent placement of children under care orders.

Magistrates retired from the court to consider the disposition of the case in one third of the observed cases. In one third of the cases they did not retire at any stage but decided the matter in court.

The time taken on the disposition stage of the case varied between a few minutes and 70 minutes. Half the cases were dealt with in less than 15 minutes. Cases where there is opposition to the order recommended by the local authority take longer than those which are unopposed (median time of 27 minutes for opposed and 12 minutes for unopposed cases) but the time taken up with submissions and reading reports is fairly standard. Again the fact of representation is of much less importance in the time taken than the existence of opposition.

Outcomes of Hearings. Care orders were made in 41 of the 47 cases in which disposal was considered. Supervision orders were made in 6 cases, 4 of them following the social worker's recommendation. The social worker's recommendation was followed by the court in all but 3 cases; in two a supervision order was made when a care order was recommended and in one a care order was made when a supervision order was recommended. This latter

was one referred to above where the social worker had wanted a care order but had asked for a supervision order because of doubts about the evidence. The child's solicitor in this case had argued strongly for a care order and the magistrates had decided that a care order should be made.

Considering both stages of the case it could be said that out of the 49 court hearings the social services 'lost' their case on only three occasions; one when the case was not proved and two when a supervision rather than a care order was made. In one of these two latter cases evidence was submitted in relation to non-school attendance and cruelty to the child. The evidence of cruelty was based on allegations made by the child and the mother which were subsequently withdrawn by them. The local authority recommended a care order. The child's solicitor submitted that the evidence on cruelty was insufficient and the non-school attendance only merited a supervision order. The magistrates, having withdrawn to consider the facts and the disposal simultaneously, agreed with the views of the child's solicitor. In the second case the evidence was not thought to be strong and the magistrates, again considering the facts and disposition together, made a supervision order. The Social Services Department was not unhappy about the order.

Several of the cases quoted above highlight the fact that in a number of hearings the proving the facts stage of the case is not distinguished from the 'disposition' stage. Supervision orders being used where a lower standard of proof applies than for a care order is a case in point. Of the 30 care proceedings we observed in which both the facts and the disposal were at issue, there were at least 12 when the two stages were not distinguished. The procedure in these cases is usually as follows: the local authority solicitor presents his case; witnesses are called, examined and cross-examined; the child's solicitor or the parents call their witnesses, if any. When the evidence is concluded the local authority solicitor makes a short statement saying that on the basis of these facts the local authority is applying for a care order and the child's solicitor also puts his view on the appropriate order. The social enquiry report is then handed to the magistrates who retire. When they return they simply announce the order on which they have decided. This procedure was followed in 7 observed cases. There are variations on this pattern, for example the magistrates may remain in court while they read the report (2 cases) or there may be no report but they still retire to consider the two stages simultaneously (1 case). In two cases the report was introduced at the beginning of the hearing before the facts were heard. There is no difficulty in determining those cases where the facts and disposition are clearly distinguished. The separation of phases may be marked by the chairman of the bench or the clerk saying whether or not they find the case proved. The bench retire at the end of both stages or the report may not be submitted until after the bench has retired after hearing the facts. The practice of allowing the two stages to merge into each other is opposed by some clerks of court who may on occasions quite firmly interrupt a magistrate who fails to make the distinction. In other courts where the clerk does not take such a strong view the merging may occur in some cases and not in others. In most of the cases we observed when the stages merged, the child was represented and neither the local authority nor the child's solicitor made any protest.

The Hearings Overall. It is not uncommon for there to be discussions and disagreements between the clerk, the bench and the solicitors about matters of procedure during a care proceedings hearing. This occurred in 23 of the 33 cases we observed. The discussion sometimes concerned relatively minor points such as whether the rule that a child who is under 5 need not be present in court means that a child should attend after its 5th birthday or not until after its 6th birthday. Sometimes there were more serious disputes. For example, in a case where an application was made to vary a supervision to a care order there was dispute as to whether the evidence which led to the supervision order could be heard or only the evidence relating to the subsequent period. The clerk of the court in this case advised the bench that the latter was the proper course despite representations from the local authority solicitor that all the evidence should be heard. (When an appeal was made to the Crown Court against the care order made in this case it was the judge's view that the advice to the bench had been mistaken.)

In some cases procedural anomalies clearly occur. We have already mentioned a number; hearing a case in the absence of the parents or a child over 5; no hearing of the facts because the case is unopposed; the social enquiry report being submitted at the beginning of the hearing; parties other than the child or parents being represented and taking part (e.g. grandparents); and the merging of the facts and disposition stages. We also observed 4 cases where a person who was later to be a witness was present in court throughout and thus heard the evidence of earlier witnesses. One or other of these anomalies occurred in nearly two-thirds of all the care proceedings we observed.

The discussion and disagreements about appropriate procedures and the observable variations and anomolies in the hearing of cases, suggest that there is a good deal of uncertainty and sometimes ignorance about the procedure in care proceedings. Of course these kinds of discussion and variations occur in all courts. However in most areas of law the anomalies are normally sorted out by appeals being made to higher courts. Case law is thus developed to guide practice in the lower courts. In care proceedings there are very few appeals and very little case law on the details of procedure. The normal standardisation mechanism is therefore not particularly effective in this area of law.

Another feature of some cases which seemed to us to be unsatisfactory was the comparatively short time taken by the hearing. It is hard to see how a serious evaluation can be made of the best interests of the child in a short time, say less than an hour. A third of the cases were in court for less than an hour and on occasions for less than half an hour. (Range of total time 5 minutes to 7 hours; mean time = 110 minutes; median time = 72 minutes.)

In summary, then, we can make an overall assessment of each of the hearings observed in the juvenile court by asking:

(a) was the laid down procedure departed from in a way which could have detracted from the fullness or fairness of the hearing?

and (b) was adequate time given to considering the case (say at least 1 hour)?

Applying these criteria to the 33 care proceedings hearings we observed in court, there were only 10 hearings which we considered satisfactory.

The social enquiry report in care proceedings

In all care proceedings under CYPA 1969 and in criminal prosecutions where the magistrates may consider making a care order on a juvenile, the local authority social services department (or probation service) has a duty to make investigations and report on the background and circumstances of the child. These reports, usually known as social enquiry reports or court reports (and shortened here to SER), are of considerable importance in both the preparation and hearing of cases in the juvenile court. These reports will be discussed here in some detail.

S. 9(1) CYPA 1969 specifies the duty to report to the court on 'such information relating to the home surroundings, school record, health and character of the person in respect of whom the proceedings are brought as appear to the authority likely to assist the court'. The Magistrates Rules (Children and Young Persons) (1970) defines the use of the reports in court (Rule 20 (1)).

The rules and statutory requirements seem to identify a straightforward procedure for providing the court with information relevant to its decision. However in observing how these procedures operate in practice there are a number of problems which arise about the proper content of reports, their use by the courts and their ownership, role and status. There are also considerable differences in attitudes to social enquiry reports between the professional groups involved in care proceedings.

In criminal cases there is a clear distinction between those parts of the proceedings concerned with proving whether an offence has been committed and the disposition of the case. The nature of the offence and what would constitute proof that it has been committed are well defined. The home background and circumstances are only considered in the disposal part of the proceedings in association with other matters such as previous convictions. In contrast, in care proceedings there can be a considerable degree of overlap in the material which is relevant in the two stages and the grounds which must be provided are much less well defined. Frequently much of the material covered in a home background report is also entered as evidence in relation to the facts. Consequently the social worker who prepares the SER may be an important, and sometimes, the only witness as to the facts. The SER in these circumstances doubles as his proof of evidence and as a document is very much more important than the report to the court in criminal cases.

In criminal cases there is a clear distinction between the agency bringing the prosecution and responsible for proving the case, and the agency reporting to the court on the background and possible disposal of the case. In care proceedings brought by the local authority there is no such distinction. The social worker is involved in the decision to bring the proceedings, in proving the facts and in reporting to the court. In these three different roles the same body of material will be drawn on and summarised in the SER. Inevitably confusions arise between these three roles both in the mind of the person carrying the roles, those with whom the person deals, and in the status and use of information.

In criminal cases there are a range of options which the magistrates may

consider in the disposition phase of the proceedings. Since there are a range of possibilities, the SER may be expected to consider the possible alternatives and offer suggestions as to their appropriateness in the case. However, in care proceedings, particularly those brought by the local authority, there may be no effective choice once the case has been found proved. The role of the SER in advising the magistrates on disposition may consequently disappear.

Each of these aspects contribute to the tendency (discussed above) for the different parts of care proceedings to merge or become confused; the similarity of the material considered in the two parts, the same people appearing in each part, the same body of material being drawn on at each stage and the lack of alternatives available once the first part has been concluded. Much of the confusion and disagreement about the role and use of the SER must be seen in this context.

Solicitors' and Social Workers' Views on the Role of the SER

Most social workers and solicitors see the SER as playing a very important role in care proceedings; 60% of solicitors in the sample held this view and 85% of social workers saw writing court reports as an important part of their job. Some solicitors saw the report as important because it contained most of the information relevant to the case. Others emphasised the importance of the report in influencing the magistrates' thinking; 13 said that magistrates rely on the SER and see it as an independent assessment. This dependence on the report of the social workers may be seen as overdependence and 11 solicitors felt that the magistrates tend to abdicate their decision to the SER and simply follow its recommendations, for example, 'Whether it is right or wrong it is regarded as a new revelation of the gospel truth by the magistrates.' Social workers tend to see the SER as a 'report for the court' and meant to assist the court in the making of a disposition; 53 said that writing SERs was important because magistrates use them and are influenced by them. Although very few social workers (12) thought that magistrates are too dependent on social workers' recommendations, many are aware that magistrates do, in general, accept the recommendations social workers put to the court.

Those who thought the SER unimportant in care proceedings were in the minority. Five solicitors said the report was not important since all the material had already come out in the hearing of the facts and therefore the SER did not add anything new. Only 12 social workers thought that writing reports was not an important part of their job and said that magistrates don't read them and ignore the recommendations.

While the importance of the SER is not in dispute for the majority of the participants, the question of what it should set out to do and what it should contain is a more contentious issue. Should it simply be a summary of the facts or should it build up an argument for a recommendation? Does it assist the court by simply providing information or does it assist by giving the court the opinion of a professional along with the evidence on which that opinion is based?

The majority of social workers (81%) believed they should try and build up an argument for the recommendation when writing a report. On the other

hand some solicitors (10) saw the SER mainly as a summary of the facts, 'a helpful summary' which 'saves time and effort' and 'gives the total picture'. Twelve thought it should be restricted to a statement of the facts. Half the sample of solicitors wanted the SER to give the full background on the case, particularly information which only the social worker is likely to have. Nine thought it should contain the social workers' opinions, feelings and conclusions about the situation. While solicitors see the value of the SER as a source of information, they are less agreed about the social workers' recommendations; 9 said the SER should contain firm recommendations, 13 that reasons and arguments for a recommendation should be given. A few, following the model from criminal cases, thought the report should consider the alternative dispositions and make an evaluation of each.

Four said that the SER should discuss what the social services intend to do with the child if a care order were obtained, what they hope to achieve and likely future developments in the case. These matters are not usually mentioned in SERs. If they were to be covered in reports they would draw attention to important aspects of the decision which the magistrates must make, namely what are the options to be decided between and what is the alternative care which the child might receive. The social worker as the professional advisor to the court is probably the person in the best position to draw attention to these matters. However, the social worker also has an interest in achieving a particular outcome and raising alternatives may diminish the likelihood of his recommendation being accepted.

In writing a SER social workers seem to make a résumé of information available from their own knowledge or from files. At worst this involves long chronological family histories. (One SER ran to 12 typewritten pages). At the other extreme the factual material contained in the report may be rather limited. Some private solicitors mentioned that SERs can be incomplete factually, (14), and some made the specific complaint that the report may be prepared by a social worker who is not familiar with the case and omits important information. Although in the majority of cases included in the study the social worker had known the family for a considerable length of time, a social worker may write a report largely from secondhand sources.

In writing a report the social worker must make a selection from the available information: some things will be included, others excluded. It is usually left to the social worker to make his own judgements as to what is appropriate, although he may receive some help from a senior, the courts officer or the local authority solicitor. Social workers in general receive little or no guidance as to what should be included in an SER other than very broad headings. There is little written material available and it is not usually dealt with in any depth in training courses. Under these circumstances it would not be surprising if sometimes there was unconscious or even conscious selectivity at work. Since the author of the report is usually involved in the decision to take proceedings (at least in those cases brought by the local authority) he can hardly be blamed for making his case as strongly as possible. To expect him to step back and make an entirely objective evaluation without very strong professional and ethical guidelines to help him is perhaps unreasonable. It is sometimes argued in defence of selectivity that the inclusion of some material

may make future relationships with the family difficult or that some information may cause unnecessary distress to the family. It may be desirable to protect people but this is not a reason for withholding the information from the court.

It is clear from the SERs we have examined that most go beyond providing extra background information. They often included opinions, assessments and interpretations. In doing so they appear to be offering the court 'professional' or 'expert' opinion. The SER could be seen as an 'expert' report and it is useful to look at SERs from this point of view. The reports of experts are often submitted to courts in civil trials (e.g. medical, psychiatric, engineering reports). These reports normally contain:

(a) the qualifications and experience of the author, to establish the author's special skills and expertise;

(b) an account of the basis of the author's opinions e.g. number and timing of observations, tests conducted, other persons consulted, files examined, etc.;

(c) the conclusions resulting from the investigations; and where relevant

(d) a prognosis for the future, including comments on treatment, etc.

An 'expert report' should not confuse fact and opinion, represent opinion as fact, use unverified information or hearsay, contain errors of fact or make imprecise statements. Above all, the court should be satisfied that it is an independent assessment by the author. It contains a professional judgement made according to professional criteria unrestricted by any external pressures.

How do social enquiry reports measure up to these criteria? First, in none of the SERs examined in cases in this study did the author clearly state his qualifications and experience. The report was put forward by the social worker as a member of the local authority with a duty to investigate, rather than as a 'professional social worker'. Second, only one SER briefly set out the data collection activities which formed the basis of the conclusions. In other reports the data base was referred to in a general way, for example, 'during the course of visits', 'contact on an informal basis', 'long history of our involvement'. In many criminal proceedings, social work involvement is requested by the court and visits are made for the sole purpose of gathering information for the SER. The information made available to the court is often recent and its source is made explicit in the report. However, in care proceedings the author has usually known the child or family for a considerable length of time. Information for the SER tends to be drawn not only from the social worker's records but from his memory and from departmental files. The files include material collected by other people or agencies who have been involved from time to time. Information may therefore have come from many different sources. Nevertheless it is rare for the source of the information included in the report to be specified. Third, nearly every SER we examined contained an example of opinions presented as facts, e.g. 'although the parents would like to have their child back home, there has been no fundamental modification of attitude on either side'. In all cases there were instances of fact and opinion being mixed up together. Many SERs, especially those written in chronological

sequence, read as convincing stories. It is very difficult to differentiate the elements which are factual and those which are opinion.

A number of solicitors commented on these aspects of SERs and some noted that reports include material which is not relevant, which cannot be challenged or does not conform to the rules of evidence. Indeed an examination of SERs shows that it is common for comments and opinions expressed by others to be included, e.g. 'This was considered unsatisfactory by all who visit there' '...we received reports that...' 'Neighbours reported that...' (Many courts seem reluctant to challenge the use of hearsay in care proceedings, even in the giving of evidence to the facts.) Some solicitors thought SERs woolly, verbose and jargon ridden (9) and the quality of SERs varies widely in this respect. Some were concise, others were indeed lengthy and verbose. While SERs may not contain as much jargon as some other specialist reports, they do include statements which are imprecise and words that are open to interpretation, e.g. 'disorganisation within the home', 'potentially volatile domestic situation', '...has been described as "feckless", "immature" and "manipulative"'. The behaviour which occasioned these statements is seldom given. Undoubtedly there are considerable difficulties involved in making a distinction between interpretations and the behavioural evidence. However, if the concepts are not explained and the behaviour not described it seems questionable whether the use of these words is desirable when addressing a lay audience.

Nearly all SERs contain a recommendation and a reason for that recommendation, although reasons vary in their depth. When recommending a care order it is usually argued that supervision will not suffice, for example because of an unco-operative parent. It is rare for the social worker to offer a prognosis for the future, or to outline what the social services intended to do with the child if a care order was made.

We have no evidence as to whether the courts accept the SER as an independent, professional assessment. There seems no reason to suppose that they do not since it is unusual for the bench to ask any questions of the social worker about the report. Solicitors however are more sceptical. 9 solicitors went so far as to say that the SER can be biased, partisan, one-sided; for example, 'The SER must be dubious if the same person who has written it also gives evidence.'; 'it is very hard for them to give reasons for their recommendations where they have to be all things to all men and maintain the relationship with the client'; 'it should be an independent report but the social worker is involved in the decision to take the proceedings and gives evidence as a local authority witness, then is supposed to make an evaluation and recommendation. They are therefore sitting in judgement on their own cases.'

It seems fairly clear that in current practice, the SER does not conform to the model of an 'expert report'. It may be that this is an inappropriate model and that some other model should be applied to social enquiry reports. It should be noted that there is a general tendency for 'experts' in the juvenile courts to behave in a less 'expert' way that would be expected in other courts. This applies to doctors, psychiatrists and psychologists as well as to social workers. Moss and Sutton (1981) have, for example, been critical of educational psychologists in the juvenile court. The lack of vigorous cross-examination and the unlikelihood of experts being called by the 'other side'

probably underlie this trend. However there is, in addition, a pervasive assumption that less professional and theoretical rigour need be applied to welfare law than when money or liberty are at stake. Some social workers mistakenly suppose that this is the implication of the standard of proof being 'balance of probability' rather than 'beyond reasonable doubt'.

In so far as SERs are used in relation to proving the facts either as the basis of the social workers' evidence, by solicitors or by the court it is desirable for the material which is factual to be clearly distinguished from opinion and interpretation. The source of the information should probably also be indicated unless it can be established that it is not in dispute. If the use of the report is confined to the disposal part of the hearing then perhaps these criteria could be more relaxed. However, in care proceedings it is extremely difficult to ensure such separation in the procedures of the court and in the minds of the participants because of the overlap of material in the two stages.

Access to the Report

The SER has a role to play outside the actual court proceedings. Some social workers mentioned for example that it is the official report of the department and may be used in appeals. It may be an aid to social work practice, helping social workers reflect on their cases (19), providing a summary for future references (5), or as a stage in the development of relationships with the client (13). Only one social worker thought the SER important because solicitors use it. Whether or not solicitors should have access to the report before the hearing is an area of great uncertainty and there are wide variations both in views and in practice. By giving the bench discretion whether or not to disclose the contents of the SER in court, the wording of the Magistrates Court Rule 20(2) tends to suggest that the intention was to restrict access to the SER. However, the rules give no indication as to the proper practice in relation to prior discussion or disclosure of the report. Although there is clearly no obligation for the social services to disclose the report prior to the hearing, there appears to be no legal restriction on them doing so.

About one quarter of social workers interviewed said that they would give a private solicitor a copy of the SER and another quarter said they would not. Many did not know what they should do. Some felt that they might give information orally, telling the solicitor the recommendation in the report (19) or the basic facts (5), but not giving him a physical copy. Some felt they would need to be sanctioned to give the solicitor the report either by their senior, area officer or local authority solicitor (11) or by the client (10). A few said that there was a rule that they should not give the solicitor a copy, although as far as we could determine no such rule existed in any of the authorities or area offices. Comments from solicitors suggest that these answers do reflect practice. For example only a quarter of solicitors said that they got the SER before the hearing and 7 reported getting the contents verbally from the social worker. A third of the solicitors said that it was usual for them to be handed the report as they went into court. Three said that they only receive a copy after the case has been proved.

In the cases we observed, access to SERs varied although it was sometimes very difficult to tell at what stage solicitors received a copy of the SER or were

informed of its content. However it seemed to be common for private solicitors to obtain a copy just before the hearing. Of course many SERs are only written 2–3 days before the hearing (12/29 known dates) or sometimes in the week just prior (3). With delays for typing, many reports are only physically available the day before the hearing. While 11 had been written up to one month before, and 3 over a month, the majority of these had been written for a previous interim care order proceeding, addendums having been attached just prior to the final hearing.

Social workers are sometimes reluctant to give a copy of the SER to solicitors because they feel that they may rely on the report rather than making their own enquiries. This attitude is widespread and on occasions may be justified. For example in one case we observed, the social worker had given the solicitor a copy of the SER before the hearing and was very annoyed that he had used it in court and had not done any investigations himself. One social worker summed up this attitude saying 'The seniors are against us giving a copy to the solicitor because that would be doing his job for him'. It is widely believed by social work staff that the SER is strictly a report for the court and therefore no-one else should see it. In one case where the solicitor had made strong requests for the report the Director of Social Services had been referred to. He had refused to provide the report because access to the SER 'was at the discretion of the court and only necessary after the case is found proven.'

Not surprisingly solicitors take another view of the matter. Recognising the importance of the SER in care proceedings some solicitors feel that without a prior opportunity to read the SER they cannot adequately represent their client (15). A few said that without it they were going into court blind. If the solicitor representing a child cannot obtain the relevant information from the social worker he must investigate the case himself. However this may not be very easy. For example, a solicitor representing the child may have difficulty in obtaining background details from the parents and the child may be too young to give information. Solicitors often say they are just too busy to investigate a case properly themselves and one said it was a 'duplication of investigative time'. In any case solicitors may not be the ideal people to interview witnesses in relation to these delicate matters. They may be unskilled in obtaining co-operation, not know what questions should be asked or how questions should best be phrased.

In terms of facilitating the hearing of the case there seem to be advantages to the solicitors having access to the report. One chief clerk stated during a case that it 'would be helpful in care proceedings if the SER was made available to solicitors as soon as possible'. He argued that if solicitors were not given copies, then they would ask for an adjournment so as to have time to rebut any allegations made in the report. Without a prior opportunity to read the report it is difficult to establish the points in dispute and, in some cases, whether there is a conflict of interest between the parents and the child. This latter issue was raised in an observed case.

Use of the SER in Court

Rule 20 of the Magistrates Courts (Children and Young Persons) Rules 1970 makes it clear that the SER should only be introduced into court when the

applicant's case has been found proved. In only 18 of the care proceedings we observed was this procedure clearly followed (including one case where the case was found not proved). In two instances the bench made an order without referring to the SER although both copies of the report and the author were present in court. In two cases the SER was introduced at the beginning of the hearing. In one case the clerk suggested that the report should be used to facilitate examination of witnesses and hence shorten the proceedings. Both the local authority solicitor and the child's solicitor agreed. The parents were not asked and subsequently said that they felt that because of this the case had been decided from the start. In a second case, the report was submitted on the suggestion of the local authority solicitor as the evidence in the case since both the representatives of the child and the parents agreed that a care order should be made. This suggestion was accepted by the clerk and the representatives and no witnesses were called. In the remaining 11 observed cases the SER was submitted after the facts had been heard but without any indication being given as to whether the case had been proved. Occasionally the clerk made the suggestion that the magistrates should have the SER while they retired to consider the facts as this would shorten the proceedings.

Under Rule 20 (2) of the Magistrates Rules (Children and Young Persons), the court is under a duty, where the report is not read aloud, to inform the infant and parent or guardian of any part of it bearing on the person's character or conduct which the court considers material to the manner in which the case should be dealt with. (The court has a discretion to disregard this duty with a child where it 'appears impractical due to his age and understanding'.) 'If such a person then desires to produce further evidence thereto, the court, if it thinks the further evidence would be material, shall adjourn proceedings for the production thereof.'

In the sample of observed cases it was usually not possible to tell if the parents had been shown the SER at some time prior to the hearing. However many social workers do make a practice of going over the content of the report with their clients before a hearing. Parents were generally shown the report during the hearing if there was a suitable adjournment after its submission, for instance, when the bench retired. This also applied to the children present who were of a 'suitable' age. In general, the social worker or the child's solicitor took the report over to the child or parents on his own initiative. If there was no suitable adjournment parents tended not to see the report. In one instance the mother was deliberately not shown the SER because the court feared her reaction to reference in it to her alleged 'schizophrenic' condition. In these instances the opportunity was lost for either child or parents to produce evidence in rebuttal. However even where the parents were shown the report or told of its contents, they usually did not call further evidence. While the social worker who wrote the SER is usually present in court to speak to the report it is rare that any questions of substance are asked by either magistrates or lawyers. Only two social workers said that in their experience magistrates always asked questions, while 51 said sometimes, 48 rarely, and 19 said that they were never asked questions by magistrates. The social worker may be asked if she has anything to add or for minor points of clarification. Only two said they were asked about facilities or resources. This parallels what was

observed in cases. In 5 instances the social worker was asked by the bench if she wanted to make comments, etc. In each, the social worker declined. In 2 cases the social worker was actually examined on the SER. In one instance, the bench, while retiring, asked questions through the clerk. On 3 occasions the legal representatives asked questions of the author. Thus it appears to be comparatively rare for information contained in the report to be checked, challenged or supplemented in court.

Conclusions

There can be little doubt of the importance of the social enquiry report in care proceedings to all the participants. Its importance and ubiquity however are not conducive to a constructive analysis of its proper content or use. Many of those interviewed or with whom the matter was discussed simply could not imagine that reporting could be handled in any other way. There are however real problems associated with the report.

(a) The social enquiry report in care proceedings covers material which may be relevant to both parts of the proceedings. For the social worker, this means that his preparation of the SER normally doubles for his preparation of his evidence as a witness to the facts and in some cases as a brief for a decision-making event such as a case conference. For the solicitor the SER is effectively the résumé of the material relevant to the preparation of his case and therefore a document which he would like to obtain. In court the duplication of material creates the temptation to take the report either before hearing the facts or while deciding on the facts. Thus the report embodies and perhaps exacerbates the tendency to confuse the two elements, both of the proceedings themselves and of the role of the social worker in the case.

(b) The SER is prepared by a member of the agency making the application. In addition the social services department is closely identified with the resource provision required as a result of the court's decision. There are thus both real and perceived problems of the independence of the report. First, there are pressures not to allow the respondent access to the report prior to the hearing as this may be felt to weaken the applicant's position. Second, the report, seen as an official report of the applicant and resource provider, may be held in excessive regard or treated with excessive suspicion by the court, solicitors and others according to their views on the power and intentions of the authority. Third, the authority making the report is also the potentially responsible agency if an order is made and there are pressures not to constrain the agency's future freedom of action by raising issues concerning the future of the child.

(c) A home circumstances report in a criminal trial can consider a range of sentencing or disposal options, although the effective choice may be limited by the circumstances of the case. In care proceedings there is little or no choice and the whole report therefore becomes an argument for a care order. The section of the report which might be concerned with an evaluation of the appropriate future of the child has in general atrophied.

All these conditions give the SER a different role in the proceedings to that of a court report in a criminal case. The latter tends to function as a plea in mitigation, entering the circumstances of the individual and humanitarian considerations to be put in the scales against punishment and the protection of society. The SER in contrast functions as a reinforcement and restatement of the applicant's case. As such it is probably carrying too heavy a burden. In its use both inside and outside the court the single document is serving too many functions. Its singularity contributes to confusions and difficulties about the role of the social worker, the distribution and status of information and the various components of the decision-making system.

Reports as they are currently written also create problems for the recipients. The presentation of unsubstantiated opinion and the lack of evaluation of alternative interpretations or options leaves those who read the report with no means of checking, challenging or evaluating the contents. They must take it or leave it. Any challenge to the report takes the form of a personal attack on its author. The dynamics of courtrooms create pressures against personal attacks of this kind and they are rare in our observation. Unless solicitors or magistrates have additional or independent evidence to draw on, there is little alternative for the court but to accept the report as offered.

Having considered the use of the social enquiry report and examined a number of reports submitted to the juvenile court, we believe that there is a good case for a 'development exercise' to be undertaken in respect of social enquiry reports. Report writing is immensely variable. Many reports can be severely criticised, particularly with reference to the criteria normally applied to reports from other experts or professionals. The published material on how to prepare a social enquiry report in relation to care proceedings is extremely limited.

A development exercise might begin by considering whether the social enquiry report should be divided into separate sections or even separate reports. As a first step it could be useful to clearly distinguish three main types of information with which the social worker is concerned.

(a) *Factual information*
   – the incidents or circumstances which led to the case being brought to court;
   – the circumstances of the family and the child;
   – actions taken by the social worker.

(b) *Interpretations*
   – assessments of family dynamics;
   – interpretations of the intention or significance of behaviour;
   – prognosis and evaluation (e.g. potential risk; child's development; likely affects on emotional life etc.)

(c) *Appropriate actions*
   – what care should be provided for the child;
   – resource availability;
   – legal protection or powers required.

The kinds of material included under each of these headings would need to be

further explored and specified. Once having developed a more structured view of the information base which should be considered in any case, the exercise could then go on to consider such questions as:

(a) how should each class of information be recorded?

(b) at what level of detail should the information of each type be reported in formal reports?

(c) which types of information should be available to
    − the court in the form of evidence,
    − the court in the form of assessments and recommendations,
    − the local authority solicitor,
    − a case conference,
    − the solicitor representing the child,
    − the parent (or his solicitor)?

(d) whether certain types of information should be circulated to all parties beforehand?

(e) whether a statement of certain facts could be agreed and submitted to the court in written form?

The aim of the development exercise would be to produce suggested formats for reporting, procedures and teaching materials to guide practitioners and for use in training students.

These are, of course, only suggestions about the kinds of matters a development exercise might consider. Anyone responsible for such an exercise would need to work closely with the social work profession, the courts and lawyers specialising in the field. Development in the techniques and skills of court reporting could have a number of benefits:

(a) a more consistent and higher quality of reporting would improve the professional standing of social work particularly with lawyers and the courts;

(b) improvements in reporting could contribute to the development of professional practice in decision-making and planning for children;

(c) work on the social enquiry report would provide a focus and a containing boundary for dealing with some important issues in relation to the complexity of social workers' roles, the relationship of social workers to the courts and information availability and confidentiality issues in relating to other parties.

Roles and role performance in care proceedings

The magistrates and the clerk

The social character of a hearing in the juvenile court can be determined by the style adopted by the magistrate or the clerk of the court. The magistrates can take an active part in asking questions of witnesses although it is usually only the chairman who does so. In 6 of the care proceedings we observed the bench

asked a number of questions and a few questions were asked in another 12 cases. However in 15 cases no questions were asked by the bench. The clerk too may sometimes ask questions in order to clarify some matter (10 cases). The chairman of the bench sometimes conducts the proceedings much in the style of a chairman of a committee, controlling and directing proceedings with only an occasional reference to the clerk. We observed cases being run in this style on 10 occasions.

Particularly in one court the chairman had been on the bench for a number of years and had strong views both on the procedure and the disposal options. In other courts both the clerk and the magistrates are active in the proceedings, sharing the activities and consulting with each other. Eight cases were observed, in three courts in particular, where the proceedings were conducted in this way. In other cases the clerk takes up a role not unlike a 'master of ceremonies', conducting and arranging proceedings for the benefit of the bench. The bench remains passive, is only nominally consulted by the clerk and the magistrates often look bemused, particularly when having to deal with points of law. Thirteen cases were conducted in this way and the style seemed characteristic of 5 juvenile courts.

The balance between the magistrates and the clerk is at least partly a matter of their respective knowledge and experience. The personality of the people involved must also contribute. The nature of any particular case will also affect the balance of roles in the court. For example, in two cases the local authority solicitor and the solicitor for the child took such an active part that between them they left little for the clerk or the magistrates to do. Thus there is no absolute correspondence between the court and the manner in which cases are handled. However either a well established tradition or a strong personality can set the tone in a particular court.

The Local Authority Solicitor

In his opening speech the solicitor normally summarises the applicant's case. In the main this is done clearly and briefly. As described above the solicitor usually calls several witnesses including the social worker to give evidence. Although the examination of the social worker by the solicitor usually proceeds fairly smoothly, misunderstandings or difficulties can occur and in about one third of the cases we observed this happening. In another 4 cases the social worker expressed dissatisfaction with her examination by the solicitor although there had been no obvious difficulty in court.

Sometimes the difficulty seems to arise over the degree of structure which the solicitor provides for the social worker in the questions he asks. With an experienced and well prepared social worker the solicitor only needs to give minimum guidance and reminders for the witness to respond with a coherent account of the relevant facts. The same technique used on an anxious or badly prepared social worker can result in a confusing or incomplete story being given. Even if she gives a perfectly satisfactory account of the facts with little guidance, a social worker will still sometimes complain vigourously about the uncertainty of the examination and the lack of help from the solicitor. In response to pressures of this kind the solicitor may attempt more structured

questioning. He then runs the risk of being accused of asking leading questions. Of course advocates vary in the skill with which they can steer a middle path between too much and too little guidance and whether or not they can adapt their style to individual witnesses. However social workers do seem to present more difficulties as witnesses than others.

In some cases ignorance of the rules of evidence on the part of social workers can cause problems, particularly in relation to hearsay and the use of notes. In others some social workers have difficulty in keeping their evidence to facts and not including interpretations and opinions. Many juvenile courts are not particularly strict about hearsay and opinion being used in evidence. In half the cases observed the social workers used hearsay and opinion while giving evidence, but this was only commented on in 4 cases and actually disallowed in 2. Undoubtedly it must be confusing if the social worker finds that it is not acceptable in a case when in other cases there has been no objection.

Social workers can also be critical of the overall presentation of the case by the solicitor, even sometimes when the social worker was not in court throughout. It is not uncommon for social workers to feel that the reasons for obtaining a care order are stronger than the evidence which is produced in court. When the solicitor is well liked or thought to be sympathetic to social work concerns then it is the law, the rules of evidence, or the clerk who are usually blamed for the evidence being restricted. If the solicitor is not so regarded then he may be the one who is thought to be at fault. Using the solicitor as a 'fall-guy' for the perceived shortcomings of the courts in this way is particularly clear when the social worker holds the solicitor to be responsible for procedural anomalies or the decisions of the clerk about interpretation of procedure.

As would be expected from the review of the attitudes of social workers to the local authority solicitor in the previous chapter, the solicitor's performance was more frequently criticised by social workers in cases in Local Authority 2. In most cases it seemed to us that the criticisms were overreactions to fairly minor misunderstandings. Similar problems occurred in cases in all the authorities but were not generally a major source of concern, particularly if a satisfactory outcome was achieved. Since in the vast majority of cases the recommendations of the local authority are accepted by the court neither any real or perceived shortcomings in the performance of the solicitor would appear to significantly affect the outcome in cases.

Social Workers

In most of the cases observed the social worker gave evidence competently and often with confidence and assurance. Some needed more guidance and help; 5 were clearly nervous and unsure and 3 were confused and did not answer the questions put in examination. In a few cases the social worker tended to use a great deal of 'jargon' and some found it difficult to answer more challenging questions put during cross-examination. Since the social worker may appear as both a witness and to speak to the report, confusion between these roles may occur when the court fails to maintain the distinction between the two parts of

the proceedings. The two roles of the social worker became confused in one third of the observed cases, for example when the social worker was asked about the reasons for recommending a care order during cross-examination on evidence.

In discussing social workers' attitudes to the court it was suggested that role conflict might contribute to anxiety about appearing in a case, as for example, when a social worker has to answer questions about a client when that client is present. The social worker may not only be embarrassed but may have to make a definite shift in his mode of relating to the client. In 5 cases it was clear to the observer that the social worker was reluctant to speak of certain matters in front of the client.

Solicitors

Observations of solicitors representing the child in 29 cases confirmed that testing the evidence put forward by the applicant by cross-examining witnesses is the most common element in the role as it is performed in court. In all but one of the cases in which the local authority called any witnesses the solicitor for the child cross-examined. However the extent of the cross-examination varied widely. In about half of the cases the questioning was largely confined to clarifying matters which had been raised or re-inforcing points by repetition. Acting in this clarifying role the solicitor did not ask questions about areas of information not previously covered nor did he challenge the answers already given. In the other half of the cases the solicitor cross-examined more systematically and throroughly; matters were cross checked, omissions were pinpointed and questions asked about the provenance of information. The solicitors following this model genuinely tested the evidence put forward by the applicant. It must however be said that the cross-examination of witnesses in care proceedings is extremely mild and polite in comparison with that in criminal trials and it is rare for the representative of the child to really challenge a witness.

In many cases the cross-examination of witnesses is the only component of the role. The solicitor for the child contributed to the case by calling witnesses himself in only 7 instances. In the absence of either the local authority or the parent calling the mother as witness it may fall to the child's solicitor to do so. This may be awkward for the solicitor particularly if there is a conflict between the parent and the child, since he may wish to cross-examine the mother rather than examine her and thus be unable to challenge what she says. Confusion about who is calling the mother and a certain amount of manoeuvring is sometimes clearly observable in this situation. The magistrates may wish to hear from the mother but neither the local authority solicitor nor the child's solicitor want to call her, although both would be happy to cross-examine. In some cases they may refuse to call the mother although the magistrates have asked them to do so.

In relation to the information presentation aspects of the role of the representative of the child:

9 solicitors confined themselves to clarifying information;
5 tested the evidence by cross-examination;

7 tested the evidence and called witnesses

and 8 took little or no part in the information presentation to the court
(including 4 where no witnesses were called by either side).

In considering the decision component of the role, namely whether or not the solicitor takes up a stance in relation to the case, we found that very few representatives of the child argued for an alternative interpretation of the facts in the case or that the applicant had not proved his case. This was observed in only 4 cases. It was also relatively unusual for the child's solicitor to oppose the local authority's recommendation (9 cases). In 5 cases the solicitor remained neutral, neither supporting nor opposing the recommendation and saying that it was not part of his role to take a position. However in 15 cases the solicitor actively supported the local authority's recommendation. Thus in 24 out of 29 cases the representative of the child did make a decision as to what he thought was in the child's best interests. In some cases, and notably the two where the solicitor agreed that there was no need to call any witnesses, the solicitor clearly had made up his mind on the proper outcome before the hearing began. Thus, despite the difficulties of obtaining instructions, most solicitors do make decisions as to what they consider to be in the child's interests.

Many solicitors argue that the ambiguities in the role can only be resolved when the parents are also represented. Although we cannot generalise from the small number of 'three-handed' cases we observed, there does on occasions appear to be some merit in this argument. For example, in one case the parents strongly opposed the application and were represented by a solicitor who argued forcibly on their behalf, calling witnesses including a psychologist. The local authority and the parents' solicitor essentially took up adversarial positions. The child's solicitor remained neutral, confining his role to clarifying matters. He played an important role in modifying the opposing positions and balancing the overall pattern of evidence. A care order was recommended and made by the court. In another example the parents were again strongly represented with their solicitor calling witnesses and arguing that the case had not been proved. The child's solicitor also adopted a clarifying role but on the evidence presented supported the local authority's recommendation. The court however found the case not proved. In two cases both the representatives opposed the local authority's recommendation and the contribution made by having two representatives was to ensure a more thorough testing of the local authority's evidence from the somewhat different points of view of the child and the parents. In the two remaining cases however, there appeared to be little advantage in two solicitors being present as both agreed with the recommendation and neither made any major contribution to the proceedings.

While observing hearings in the juvenile court the observer made a subjective assessment of the overall performance of solicitors representing children and parents. In making an assessment a number of aspects were taken into account. In four cases the solicitor made no contribution to the proceedings. In seven cases the solicitor appeared to be badly prepared and have little or no information about the case and in 4 the solicitor depended entirely on the social enquiry report for his information. Some solicitors, and more particu-

larly barristers, adopted an aggressive or hostile form of cross-examination which seemed unacceptable to the court, on occasions eliciting open irritation or reprimands from the bench or the clerk. On at least two occasions advocates were clearly unfamiliar with the relevant law and procedure. Using these criteria one third of the solicitors were judged by the observer to give a less than satisfactory performance. One third were satisfactory and another third were rated as representing the client well, taking an active and effective part in the proceedings.

It is interesting to note that all the solicitors who impressed the observers came from the non-metropolitan authorites. Solicitors who had difficulty with the role came from each of the authorities but the number was proportionally higher in the two metropolitan areas. This finding is contrary to the popular belief that because legal expertise is concentrated in the main metropolitan centres that better legal services are available in these areas in the general way. In provincial cities and towns the tendency for a small number of individual solicitors to specialise in juvenile court work and for cases of this type to be directed to them seems to result in representation of better quality being available in the normal run of cases.

Social workers involved in cases sometimes expressed concern about the part played by solicitors in the hearings (7 cases). However their criticisms tended not to co-incide with those of the observer. They were largely directed at solicitors representing the child who had actively opposed the local authority's case. This seems to reflect an implicit assumption made by a number of social workers that the solicitor representing the child will agree with the social worker if he is, like her, considering the interests of the child. A solicitor who opposes is assumed to have been captured by the parent. Only in one instance did a social worker express concern that the child's solicitor had agreed with the local authority's case and had not been active in testing the evidence. The general absence of criticism of this kind is consistent with the hypothesis that social workers do not in general see the importance of the court hearing as an opportunity for an objective and independent review of the case. In the interviews with social workers only 19/150 mentioned that an advantage of representation was to put the local authority case to the test and consequently to ensure that all the facts came out in court.

The part played by parents

In the 24 observed cases where the parent (or other main contender for the care of the child) was present but was not represented the parent took an active part in the proceedings in 10 cases. In 8 cases the parent cross-examined the local authority witnesses; in 8 the parent addressed the court and in 4 called and examined his own witnesses. In 6 cases the parent took no part despite being asked if he wished to ask questions, call witnesses or address the court. In 8 cases the parent took no part and no opportunity was given for him to do so. It seemed to be normal practice not to encourage the parents to take part in two courts in particular although this occasionally happened in other courts as well. In 6 of these 8 cases the parent was called as a witness by either the local authority or the child's solicitor so that the court had information on the views of the parents in this way.

It is of course, very difficult for an unrepresented parent to make a significant contribution in a court hearing. Many have difficulty expressing their views in this formal context and the conventions of asking questions of witnesses are unfamiliar to them. In some cases (6) the clerk gave the parent some assistance, for example in rephrasing questions or by assisting when the parent wished to give evidence on his own behalf. While in many courts the parent is allowed to take a greater part than merely 'rebutting allegations' made against him, as specified in the procedural rules, their contribution is usually severely limited by their lack of verbal skills and unfamiliarity with court procedure and language.

Cases involving other proceedings

1. Opposed S2 resolutions

The local authority may decide to pass a resolution under S2 1948 Children Act vesting parental rights in the authority. Such resolutions can only be passed in respect of children already in care under S1 of the Act. The procedure is not therefore a means of removing children from undesirable homes but it does allow the local authority to resist a parent's demands for a child's return when this is considered undesirable. It can also be used as a means of the local authority obtaining powers in order to make arrangements for the long term care of the child.

Parents who will be affected by a resolution can give their consent in writing before the resolution is passed. Unless they do so the Local Authority must give notice that the resolution has been passed and of the parents' right to object. Counternotice must be served by the parent within one month. The resolution then automatically lapses after 14 days or the local authority can refer the case to the juvenile court. At the court hearing the local authority as complainant has to prove the existence of the grounds specified in the resolution, both at the time the resolution was passed and at the time of the hearing. The parent is the respondent and the court must decide whether or not the resolution should lapse.

It is comparatively rare for a parent to oppose the passing of a S2 resolution. If they do oppose then the local authority may need to go to the juvenile court. Cases of this type were included in the study where they arose during the study period (3 cases). Even when the parent has served a counternotice on the local authority, normally after having consulted a solicitor, the case may still not come to court. Of the 3 cases only one was fully heard. In the other 2 cases opposition was withdrawn. In one instance this happened just before the hearing and in the other the case was adjourned *sine die* as the mother did not turn up at the hearing having left the country. Cases where opposed resolutions are heard by the juvenile courts seem to be very rare.

The decision to take a S2 resolution rather than using some other procedure is quite straightforward in most cases. When the child has been in voluntary care for some time there is little doubt that this is the correct procedure to use. If however, the child is received into care as part of, or during the decision process there can be some confusion. There has also been some doubt over the

use of the procedure when the child is in voluntary care but the parent has given notice of his intention to remove the child following the decisions in Johns v. Jones (1978, *Family Law*. 8.5.139) and subsequent cases. None of the observed cases involved this issue. In view of conflicting decisions local authority solicitors are probably trying to avoid the problem until the legal position has stabilised.

To illustrate the circumstances of the decision to use the procedure the cases included in the sample are briefly described:

Case A: The parents in the case were separated and the mother had left the child (aged 6 years) with the father. The father could not care for the child and she was received into voluntary care and placed in a nursery. In the following months the mother intermittently demanded the return of the child. The style and insecurity of the mother's life and her poor relationship with her child were thought so unsuitable for the child that the local authority resisted the return of the child. The decision was taken to pass a S2 resolution. The father signed the consent form but the mother did not. After taking legal advice the mother served a counternotice and arrangements were made by the local authority to take the case to the juvenile court. On the morning of the hearing the social worker was informed that the mother had gone abroad and the case was adjourned *sine die*.

Case B: Two children (aged 11 and 7 years) had been in voluntary care for 3 years, placed first in a nursery and then in a small group family home. The parents were divorced. The mother spent periods in a psychiatric hospital and had no stable home suitable for caring for the children. The social services wished to arrange long term foster placements for the children and it was decided to obtain S2 resolutions. On receipt of the notice of the resolutions the mother instructed a solicitor to oppose them. The matter was referred to the juvenile court. However the mother was again admitted to hospital and the opposition was withdrawn just before the hearing.

Case C: The mother had on several occasions abandoned her illegitimate child (aged 2 years) with various relatives including her mother-in-law. The mother-in-law had a history of mental illness and the social services became concerned about the child's care. The mother-in-law was asked to place the child in voluntary care. It was decided that, as soon as the child was placed in care, parental rights should immediately be assumed. This was done with the resolution being passed verbally using a special procedure on the day the child was received into care. After consulting a solicitor the mother requested the return of the child and notified the local authority of her opposition. The matter was given a full hearing by the juvenile court.

In this last case the child had not been in voluntary care for any period when the resolution was passed, in contrast to the other two cases. At the time there may not have seemed to be sufficient evidence to justify taking a place of safety order as a means of securing the child's safety. However the social services concurrently received a referral from a GP saying that the child was losing weight and was considered to be at risk. There was however, no decision to change the procedure.

A similar confusion occurred in a case in which it was decided to take a place of safety order and subsequently care proceedings. During the period of the place of safety order the parent agreed to the child being taken into care. The local authority solicitor withdrew the application at the court and later applied for a S2 resolution. In these cases it could be argued that the wrong procedure was used, or in the second case, continued with. Since the crucial issue in bringing proceedings under S.2 C.A.1948 is whether the child is in voluntary care under S.1, there may be ambiguities about when S.1 care begins just as there has been debate about when it ends (i.e. whether the parent giving notice of his intention to remove the child terminates S.1 care). Eekelaar (1977) also noted the uncertainties which may arise in the appropriate procedures to use when children move from temporary to permanent care.

The decision-making in the 3 cases was handled within the local authority and did not involve inter-agency liaison or meetings. The local authority solicitor was involved in the decision in all 3 cases and would have drafted the form of the resolution to go to the committee. In all cases the mother consulted a solicitor but in the first two cases the solicitor's role was largely confined to serving the counternotice on the local authority. In the third case the solicitor contacted the social worker who supplied him with information about the case and only then did he serve notice of opposition. He also represented the mother at the hearing.

At the court hearing there was considerable discussion between the clerk and the solicitors as to the appropriate procedure for the case. It was agreed to introduce the social enquiry report at the outset and for the contents to be taken as the local authority's case. There was a short adjournment while the magistrates read the report. The social worker then affirmed the report and was cross-examined on it by the mother's solicitor, and re-examined by the local authority solicitor. The local authority called the health visitor and the probation officer as witnesses. The mother's solicitor called the mother. The mother's solicitor summed up and the local authority solicitor made a number of mainly legal points. The bench retired and returned to confirm the resolution. The hearing lasted for 2 hours and both parties had ample opportunity to put their case.

2. Applications for discharge of a care order

The decision-making process in proceedings to vary or discharge a care order under S 21 1969 CYPA follow a similar pattern to other types of proceedings. A decision about the appropriate care of the child must be made by the social services, information must be collected, the case prepared and presented in the juvenile court. The proceedings may be initiated either by the parent, the child or the local authority and therefore the local authority may be either the applicant or the respondent. There are also other procedural differences but these legal aspects should not obscure the essential similarities in the decision-making process and the roles performed. Cases of this type were included in the sample and 6 were identified during the study period.

There is a good deal of uncertainty about the use of discharge proceedings. The non-implementation of the amendments to the 1969 CYPA made in the 1975 CA has caused some confusion; in particular the role of the parents, their

representation and the availability of legal aid; the guardian ad litem provisions; and the appropriate court procedure. There is also uncertainty about the criteria which the court will use in relation to a case. There are no specified grounds to be proved and the CYPA only specifies that the court has to decide whether it is 'appropriate' to discharge the order and be satisfied that 'the child will receive the care and control he needs' (S.21). Since the proceedings are rarely used there has been little opportunity to establish operational definitions of these general guidelines. Magistrates must be perplexed as to how these cases should be decided and neither the applicants nor the respondents can have much idea as to how the court will react in a given case.

There are a number of circumstances in which applications to vary or discharge a care order seem to be made. The 1969 CYPA specifies that an application to discharge an order can be made 3 months after the care order has been made and every 3 months thereafter. Thus a parent who was opposed to the care order being made can effectively ask for a reconsideration of the case every 3 months. It must however be extremely rare for such an application to be successful since the family circumstances are unlikely to have changed significantly in such a short time. We found no current cases of this type. Secondly, the parent may seek to have the order discharged if, perhaps after a year or so, he is dissatisfied with the care which the child is receiving from the local authority. We found two cases of this type; one where a 14 year old girl repeatedly absconded from a community home in order to return to her father's and siblings' homes (case A); in another the mother of a 15 year old girl was dissatisfied with the care provided by a local authority home (case B). Thirdly, a child on a care order may have been returned home and have been living with its parents for several years. If the social services are satisfied with the care it is receiving they may agree with the parent that the care order should either be discharged or varied to a supervision order. This occurred in two cases; one where a child of 9 had been at home for 4 years having been originally removed because of non-accidental injury (case C); and a second where a 7 year old had been living at home for 2 years having been neglected 3 years earlier (case D). Fourthly, it may occasionally happen that a relative of the child becomes available to care for the child and applies for discharge of the care order. For example, a case where the father had returned from overseas and wished to care for the child (case E).

In one additional case (case F) the procedure was invoked by a parent who wanted more access to a child who was in the care of the local authority under a S2 resolution. The fact that the parent was principally concerned with access was not clarified before the court hearing. At the court a duty solicitor advised the mother to apply to the High Court as access was not a matter with which the juvenile court could deal.

In the 2 cases (C and D) which had involved non-accidental injury or neglect the original case conference members were consulted about the decision to discharge the order. In one the case conference was reconvened and in the other the members were contacted individually. Since the child had in each case been at home for some time and the social services were satisfied with the arrangements no objection was raised but in both cases the conference members recommended that a supervision order should be sought. In the cases where

the parents were dissatisfied with the care of the child case conferences were also held. Where the child was absconding (A) it was agreed to try a home placement. When this placement failed the application was withdrawn. In the second case (B) the conference members strongly recommended that the local authority should oppose the application. In the case where the father returned from abroad (E) the social worker supported the father in his intention to care for the child and the social services made the application.

In all 6 cases the parents consulted a solicitor at some stage on their own or on the child's behalf. The question of the representation of the child and the parent and the appointing of a guardian ad litem was handled somewhat differently in each case (excluding the instance where the application was withdrawn).

Case B: The mother made the application for discharge on behalf of the child and obtained representation for the child. The child was represented by a barrister in court. The question of the separate representation of the mother was not raised. Representation was therefore handled in the same way as care proceedings.

Case C: The social services made the application for discharge with the parents' agreement. Since the case was unopposed and had involved non-accidental injury to the child in the past, a member of the local probation service was appointed as guardian ad litem. After investigations he decided to oppose the discharge and the local authority solicitor asked for the proceedings to be adjourned *sine die* since the child was living at home in any case.

Case D: The mother made the application on the child's behalf. The clerk of the court asked the social worker to arrange legal representation for the mother. However the mother had already contacted a solicitor. The social worker arranged for the child to be represented. The child's solicitor decided that it was not necessary to appoint a guardian ad litem. Both the mother and the child were represented in court.

Case E: The social services made the application for discharge. The local authority solicitor raised the question of a guardian ad litem. The clerk of the court asked to see the social enquiry report and on that basis decided that it was not necessary to appoint one. Neither the father nor the child was represented at the court hearing.

Case F: The parents consulted a solicitor on the recommendation of the social worker and applied for discharge on the child's behalf. At court the parents had decided not to have a solicitor but the social worker urged them to contact the duty solicitor. The duty solicitor recommended that the case be adjourned and an application made to the high court.

In some of these cases there was considerable discussion between the local authority solicitor, the clerk and the private solicitors on appropriate representation. In the one case where a guardian ad litem was appointed the difficulty in obtaining a suitable independent person was apparent. The probation officer who was appointed came from the same department as the probation officer who had contact with the father in respect of his conviction

for the injuries to the child. The social services department was not satisfied that the probation officer had made an independent assessment of the situation as it now existed. The probation officer opposed the view taken by the social worker and the case conference that the care order should be varied to a supervision order. Consequently the proceedings were adjourned. It could however be argued that this is an example of the way the guardian ad litem provision was supposed to work. When the family and the social services are co-operating and are in agreement a third person should take an outside view on the child's behalf. He may not agree with the social worker and the family that discharging the order is desirable.

The procedure followed in court on the three occasions cases were heard was different in each case. Prior to each hearing the solicitors and the clerk discussed and agreed an appropriate procedural order for the case given the witnesses that the parties wished to call and the positions being taken.

Case B: The mother was the applicant and was not represented. The child was represented by a barrister with a solicitor present. The local authority was represented by a back-up solicitor. The parents and the child were present at the hearing and the courts officer and area officer attended from the social services. The child's counsel stated at the outset that he was supporting the mother's application. The mother was invited to state her application, was examined by the child's representative and cross-examined by the local authority solicitor. The counsel for the child called the child and the father as witnesses. The local authority opposed the application and called the headmistress and the area officer as witnesses. Both representatives actively cross-examined the witnesses and the mother asked questions of the local authority witnesses. The facts stage was completed by the child's solicitor addressing the court followed by the local authority solicitor. The magistrates retired and on return dismissed the application. No reports were therefore submitted. The magistrates took an active part in the proceedings asking a number of questions. The clerk dealt with procedure. The hearing took 3½ hours.

Case D: The mother was the applicant and was represented by a solicitor. The child was also represented but the local authority was not. Both parents were present. The child (aged 6½) was not present. Only the social worker attended from the social services department. The mother's solicitor stated the application and called the mother to give evidence. She was cross-examined by the child's solicitor and the magistrates. The child's solicitor declined to put an opposition case. The magistrates called the father and asked him a number of questions. The magistrates retired taking with them the social enquiry and medical reports. When the magistrates returned the child's solicitor called the social worker to ask about the alternative orders. He then stated that he was recommending that a supervision order be made. The mother's solicitor addressed the court saying the mother would accept a supervision order. The social worker was again called to speak to the report and the child's solicitor summed up. The magistrates then dismissed the application. The magistrates took an active part in questioning witnesses. The hearing took 1½ hours.

Case E: The local authority was the applicant but was not represented. The father and the child were both present, neither represented. The courts officer

and the social worker were present. At the outset the social enquiry report was submitted and taken as the facts in the case. The social worker spoke to the report and the magistrates asked the father a number of questions. The clerk called the child to ask his views. The care order was revoked and the case took ½ hour.

Obviously we cannot generalise about discharge proceedings on the basis of 3 cases. However it is worth noting a number of points about these hearings. In all three the magistrates took an active part and conducted the proceedings in almost an inquisitorial style. That is, they appeared to take seriously the requirement to satisfy themselves as to the care the child would receive. Second, the role of the child's representative seems even more obscure in these proceedings than in care proceedings particularly when a guardian ad litem is not appointed. Third, the use of the SER in cases D and E as a summary of the facts as well as a report relating to disposition parallels the problems observed in the use of these reports in S.1 proceedings.

3. Cases heard in the high court

In certain circumstances the wardship jurisdiction of the high court is invoked in child care cases. For instance, it may be used by the local authority to obtain or retain the care of a child when neither care proceedings nor passing a S.2 resolution are suitable procedures. It may also be used where the local authority's powers are not adequate to protect a child or when an authority believes that a juvenile court has inappropriately discharged a care order. Other parties including parents, relatives or friends can also invoke the jurisdiction, for example to challenge a local authority's decisions or actions in respect of a child in care or to secure a child's removal from care. The high court jurisdiction may also be used as opposed to that of the juvenile court when orders have already been made by the high court concerning a child, e.g. custody orders.

Potentially therefore, in certain cases, wardship offers an alternative procedure to those already discussed. However the jurisdictional boundaries are unclear and have been affected by a series of decisions, notably re D (a minor) (Justices decision: review. 1977. 2. *World Law Reports* 1006) and re H (a minor) (see *Family Law*. 1978.8.4.103–105). The high court has made it clear that although its jurisdiction has not been ousted by the statutory procedures, wardship should not be used as an alternative to normal procedures or as an appeal against juvenile court decisions. It is however appropriate to use wardship where there are gaps in the statutory scheme or when there are exceptional circumstances. These exceptions appear to give very wide discretion in the use of wardship. Just how wide was demonstrated by a case included in the sample in which the local authority challenged the use of the jurisdiction. In giving judgment Hon. Sir J. P. Comyn maintained that the high court could and should use its jurisdiction because the circumstances of the case were such as to give him concern regarding the welfare of the child. He went on to comment that there was considerable confusion because of the wide range of statutory law and because of the diversity of case law on the matter of jurisdiction.

Whether the high court jurisdiction is necessary to supplement the deficiencies of the statutory schemes or whether it provides a means of circumventing the intentions of the Acts is a matter of some debate. Both local authority solicitors and private solicitors have differing views on whether the wardship jurisdiction is necessary and several echoed Comyn's wish that the jurisdictional issues should be clarified.

Of the 9 wardship cases included in the sample, 5 raised the question of the use of the jurisdiction. In the other 4 cases application was made to the high court because of other orders made by the court in respect of a child or its siblings.

Case A: The local authority applied for wardship of a child of a single unsupported mother living in a mother and baby home. It was thought that the mother was not able to provide adequate care and that the child was not developing normally. The local authority solicitor recommended the use of wardship because of the difficulties involved in proving grounds under S.1 CYPA 1969 and the need to look at the overall welfare of the child.

Case B: The local authority applied for wardship of a baby newly born to a mother who had previously abandoned a child. Wardship was thought appropriate because of the difficulties in proving that a child in hospital would be 'at risk' if the mother removed it.

Case C: Wardship was initially invoked by the child's grandmother to prevent a child being sent abroad. The local authority continued to use the jurisdiction because it was believed that the relevant evidence would be admissable in the high court but not in the juvenile court. The high court agreed that this was a proper use of wardship as a supplement to the statutory system.

Case D: The solicitor for the mother, with the support of the local authority, applied for wardship. The circumstances of the case were argued to be exceptional because of medical and psychiatric issues in relation to the mother. It was also thought that the professional resources available to the high court should be used and the Official Solicitor be appointed to protect the interests of the child.

Case E: The father applied for wardship because he was dissatisfied with actions being taken in respect of his child who was in care, including her being sent abroad on a holiday. The local authority challenged the jurisdiction because there was a care order on the child and the father was seeking to interfere with the exercise of the local authority's powers. The court decided that it could exercise its jurisdiction because of concern for the welfare of the child.

Lowe and White (1979) summarise the use of wardship under four headings:

(a)   as an original jurisdiction, particularly to resolve inter-parental disputes and especially where there is a threat to remove the child from the country. (Cases C and E have aspects of this use);

(b)   as a jurisdiction of review in respect of the decisions of other bodies;

(c)   as a supplementary jurisdiction (cases A, B and C were argued to fall outside the statutory schemes);

(d)   as a fail safe or 'long stop' jurisdiction for unusual or complex cases (Case D was argued to be of this kind).

Because the statutory provisions specify particular grounds which must be proved for an order to be made, it can be argued that the high court provides a general protection for a child in circumstances which are outside the criteria, for example when the cause for concern is the future rather than the present care of the child. Lowe and White (op cit) argue in favour of the flexibility and informality of wardship unencumbered as it is by statutory constraints. There are also other ways in which the high court may be seen as providing a supplement to the statutory provisions particularly in relation to matters such as representation, rules of evidence, procedures and dispositional options. Applications to the high court may in fact be made more for these reasons than jurisdictional ones, as in cases C and D.

In the following section wardship cases are discussed with reference to aspects of the procedure which are in marked contrast to the statutory procedures. These aspects are often cited as ways in which the wardship procedure is superior to the juvenile court. Whether in practice the theoretical advantages are sustained is a matter of some doubt. For the discussion we will draw on information gathered on 9 cases in the sample, in 6 of which the court hearings were observed. Solicitors and social workers were also asked about their views of high court cases. About three quarters of the solicitors had experience of these cases but only 18% of social workers had ever been involved in a case in the high court.

(a)   *Parties and representation.* Any person who is concerned with the welfare of a child can initiate wardship proceedings. Any person may become a party to the proceedings and be represented. The Official Solicitor may be appointed to represent the child. In certain circumstances this flexibility should complement the restrictions in the statutory procedures on who can be involved. It should ensure that whoever is concerned in the care of the child puts his view to the court and has his particular point of view represented. The interests of the child can then be separately considered by the Official Solicitor. To assist him in making an assessment of the child's situation the Official Solicitor can call on appropriate professional expertise. Arrangements of this kind would seem to solve many of the problems of representation which arise in the juvenile court and are perhaps sensible and just.

Despite the difficulties experienced with representation in the juvenile court and the widespread feeling that parents should be represented and entitled to legal aid, only 2 solicitors and no social workers mentioned parties and representation as being an advantage of high court proceedings. Only 2 solicitors made reference to the Official Solicitor, one saying that his report made the hearing redundant. The local authority was represented in all of the 9 cases, mostly by the local authority solicitor and once by a barrister. The parent was represented in 7 cases; in 4 cases by a solicitor, in 2 by a barrister and in 1 by the Official Solicitor. The parent was present but not represented in 1 additional case. The Official Solicitor was appointed to act for a mother who

was mentally ill. He was also appointed to act for the child in 5 cases. In only one case did a solicitor represent the child in a way comparable to the juvenile court. The grandparents took part in 3 cases, each time being heard but not represented.

The role of the representative in high court is often rather different to his role in the juvenile court. In the juvenile court a large part of the role is as advocate during the court hearing. In the high court there is occasionally a major point of law at issue and counsel instructed to argue the point. The legal expertise element and case preparation elements of the solicitor's role are then more significant. In other cases, the representative acts as a negotiator in a civil case, using the documentary evidence available in order to negotiate a settlement which is satisfactory to his client, or at least which is the best he believes can be obtained on behalf of his client. In this role the out-of-court decision elements of the role are even more significant than in the juvenile court. However they are usually exercised on behalf of an adult rather than a child.

(b) *Evidence.* The most significant difference between the high court and the juvenile court in relation to evidence is that in the high court written evidence is submitted in the form of affidavits or reports. In contrast to the juvenile court there is disclosure of documents so this written evidence is available to all the parties prior to the hearing. The evidence is not restricted to proving specific grounds so any evidence relevant to the case can be submitted. The court can also require that specialist reports are prepared.

Several solicitors mentioned these aspects of the high court proceedings as being preferable to the situation in the juvenile court since the details of the case can be obtained in advance and the reports examined. Documentary evidence was submitted in all 9 cases; court welfare officers' reports were requested and submitted in 7 cases; medical and psychiatric reports in one case.

In relation to juvenile court hearings it is argued that the availability of information and reports before a hearing would allow a more thorough examination of the case in court. In high court hearings the effect of the availability of documents is often to reduce the hearing to a formality. On the basis of the written information, the parties negotiate an agreed arrangement before going to court. This happened in 7 of the 9 wardship cases.

The ability of the court to order expert reports appears to be a strength of the high court proceedings. In practice the advantages are less obvious. A report prepared by a court welfare officer or the Official Solicitor, as opposed to a S.E.R. prepared by the social worker in the case, should have the advantage of being clearly independent of the applicant. However independent people who have the expertise to make the assessments are not readily available, particularly outside London. In several of the cases in the study the arrangement was felt by the social worker to be unsatisfactory either because there were considerable delays in someone being available to make investigations, the investigations were thought to be superficial and based on only one visit, or made by a local probation officer who was relatively inexperienced. In one case the delay in the availability of the report was so long

that the local authority solicitor and the parents' solicitor came to an agreement without waiting for the report.

(c) *Speed.* It is sometimes argued that the wardship procedure has the advantage of an action which comes into immediate effect without prejudice. Several solicitors who were particularly concerned with the *ex parte* nature of the place of safety order procedure saw this as a real advantage of wardship. In the 9 cases in the sample there were only 2 where this feature of wardship was used, both in cases where a relative took action to prevent a child being sent abroad. In 3 other cases where emergency action was needed to protect a child, a place of safety order was taken and the wardship jurisdiction only subsequently invoked. Once the initial action has been taken to protect a child the time which elapses until a final disposition is made is very much longer in wardship cases than in those heard in the juvenile court; 4 cases took a year or longer to settle.

(d) *Decisions and disposition.* The advantages of wardship cases most frequently commented on by both solicitors and social workers were the expertise with which all the issues in the case were gone into and the flexibility of the decisions which were then made. In those cases where the case was fully heard the thoroughness of the examination of relevant matters was unquestionable. However this only occurred in 2 cases. In the other cases the court's role was confined to scrutinising the wording of a negotiated agreement and establishing that it was in fact agreed. The decisions which were reached by the court were all tailor-made to the individual cases. The range of provisions were detailed and varied. This was in stark contrast to the all-or-none nature of the orders made in the juvenile court. Examples of the decisions are:

Case A: The local authority was awarded care of the child but the mother was to attend a special unit for rehabilitation with her child.

Cases B and E: The local authority was given custody of the child with strictly defined access for the parents.

Case F: The local authority was given a care order for 6 months followed by a supervision order for 6 months with the children to return to the parents with close supervision by the local authority during the rehabilitation period.

Case G: The case concerned three children. One remained a ward residing at home; a second was made the subject of a supervision order and was to attend a child guidance clinic; and the third was to remain in the care of the local authority with a placement to be found in a special school.

The additional feature of the decisions was that the parties could apply to the court to vary the decisions if they were found not to be working. This was made explicit in several cases, particularly those where access was specified.

In practice, in the cases studied the flexibility of the decisions made by the high court was the main advantage of the wardship jurisdiction. The range of alternatives and the possibility of reviewing decisions gives the court much greater powers and relevance to the real problems of making arrangements for the care of children.

Chapter V   Conclusions

At various points in the discussion findings and observations have been reported which should be considered in an evaluation of the overall system. Suggestions have also been made about possible areas for development. In this final chapter these points are brought together in a review of the system and its effects.

This project is essentially a descriptive study of a complex system as it operates in relation to a particular set of decisions about the care of children, namely decisions about varying parental rights which must be made or ratified by a court. Gathering data in a number of different ways and from various sources we have investigated the part played by some of the main participants in the system, particularly solicitors and social workers. The task of describing was approached from an applied social science perspective. This meant giving special attention to aspects of the system which create uncertainty or friction. The study could be thought of as a diagnostic survey of an operating system. The system was observed and described as systematically and objectively as possible, but without ignoring occasional or subjective observations. The data was analysed, again as systematically and objectively as possible and an evaluation made of aspects of system functioning.

In evaluating the performance of an operating system the more formal scientific techniques are simply not available. Experimental methodologies are usually out of the question, for example, randomized treatment trials cannot be used when the care of individual children is at stake. Statistical methods are often impractical: it is too expensive and would take too long to gather a sufficiently large sample of cases to be able to statistically define the contribution of the large number of interacting determinants. In practice more indirect methods of assessment must be used. This can be done by asking a number of questions:

(a) *Does the system work as it is supposed to work?*
The decision-making system in relation to taking children into care is governed by statute, common law and by rules of legal procedure. It is carried out by organisations that are also governed by law, policy or administrative guidelines. The system, at least in some of its particulars, is supposed to work in a particular way. Identifying when it does not do so and enquiring into why not, is an important diagnostic and evaluative technique.

(b) *Are there any instances of system failure?*
At an overall level there are very few identifiable system failures. The failure to remove a child from its parents when the child is subsequently physically harmed is perhaps the only example. In other circumstances the effects on the welfare of the child of removing it or not removing it from its parents are

much more difficult to assess. However system failures can also be identified as occurring at particular points in the system. For example, information may not be communicated, arrangements may not be made, delays may occur. Because the system is complex these minor failures are usually identified and corrected. Even when such failures are infrequent or apparently trivial, establishing where and why they occur can be useful in diagnosing weaknesses in the system.

(c) *What informal system developments have occurred to supplement the formal system?*
The laws and the procedures which define the system give rise to a series of tasks and roles to be performed by individuals and agencies. Since the definition can never be complete it is necessary for operators to develop an informal system which provides more detailed specifications of roles and tasks. Further procedures may also be needed to govern the relationships between the operators. If in a number of independent locations the system has needed to be supplemented in the same area then there may be a case for more formal arrangements to be made to an aspect of the system which is deficient. Alternatively informal systems can be formally recognised. The overall variability in informal arrangements may also be an important indicator of system effectiveness. In addition the spontaneous occurrence of different informal subsystems or procedures allows some comparison to be made of their relative success.

(d) *Do the participants experience any difficulty in operating the system?*
Since the system is operated by individuals and groups we can ask whether they experience uncertainty or difficulty in using the system. Participants may express only generalised dissatisfaction or difficulty; they may be able to pinpoint areas in which difficulties occur or they may be able to analyse the aspects of the system which are unsatisfactory. All these views give important diagnostic indications even when they are expressed by a few individuals.

(e) *Are there aspects of the way the system functions which are unsatisfactory in the light of given criteria?*
Defining criteria against which the system could be evaluated is useful in a diagnostic exercise. How far such criteria are acceptable is a matter of policy or of the acceptance of research findings from other fields. For example, the criteria 'justice should be seen to be done' can be used in evaluating any legal machinery. The criteria of 'continuity of relationships and placement' can be considered in evaluating the care provided for children. It is not the function of an investigation of a system to assess the relative merits of the criteria. It is however useful to consider the data collected in relation to these criteria.

Throughout this research project we have used these kinds of questions to direct our attention to particular aspects of the system. They have also guided the organising and selecting of data to be included in this report. The report also includes purely descriptive material of how the system functions in 5 particular local authorities. In the following review of the main topics of the discussion the focus is on a diagnostic assessment of the system. Where possible we have also made suggestions for future developments or change.

The juvenile court

A hearing in court is the end point of the decision-making process considered in this project and in most cases it was the juvenile court which made (or could have made) the decision about a case. Since the earlier phases of the decision-making process are conducted with the court in mind as the final arbiter, the way the court works influences the operation of the earlier stages. The functioning of the juvenile court is therefore central to the whole system; the decisions made, the roles, and the relationships between the participants.

The review of the physical setting of the juvenile courts visited during the study showed that some courts are held in settings which are not ideal. In terms of the Home Office guidelines, the waiting areas are often inadequate. In a number of courts the waiting areas are crowded and poorly equipped with facilities such as seating, refreshments and rooms for consultation. They often lack information systems such as notice boards or enquiry desks. Occasionally the waiting areas are dirty and poorly decorated. It is not unusual for criminal and care cases to be heard on the same day and for people to wait for both types of cases in the same area. Large, formal magistrates courts are still used in some places for care proceedings. These courtrooms are intimidating to those unfamiliar with them and carry strong associations with punishment. At a practical level, it is often difficut to hear what is being said in these courts.

People involved in care proceedings may have to wait for some time for a case to be heard. They may spend more time in the waiting area than they do in court. Relatively minor improvements in the decoration and facilities could, in some courts, make a significant difference to the experience of going to court for parents, children, witnesses and professionals. Scheduling care proceedings for separate days or at least for specified times would also be desirable to minimize the mixing of people waiting for criminal cases and care proceedings. Those courts where the physical setting is more suitable, reasonably well equipped and well organized create quite a different impression. Periods of waiting can be not unpleasant and even provide useful opportunities for discussion.

The CYPA 1969 and the Magistrates Court Rules (Children and Young Persons) (1970) lay down relatively clear guidelines on how care proceedings should be conducted. They are not, however, always conducted in this way. It is rare for the 'care and control' test to be separated in any way from proving one of the specified grounds. It is also not uncommon for the two stages of 'proving the case' and 'disposition' to merge into each other. The social enquiry report, for example, may be introduced before the case is found proved. The failure to keep the different stages or legs distinct seems to arise because of the overlap between the information relevant to the different parts of the proceedings. This is further reinforced by the fact that it is the social worker who provides most of the information in both parts. Practical considerations such as the shortage of court time, the effort involved in obtaining witnesses and the cost of professional time also create pressures to eliminate repetition and to shorten proceedings. Since the limited options available to the court (see below) effectively reduce the decision of the court to whether or not to make a care order, the preservation of the two stages appears to intro-

duce unnecessary duplication which can be eliminated, for example by establishing whether the case is opposed at the outset. Thus there are both structural and practical features of the system which create pressure towards merging the two parts of the procedure. If this trend is to be counterbalanced, we would argue that real changes would have to be made and that verbal injunctions to follow laid down procedure would only be likely to have any effect in the short term.

The main variability in the way care proceedings are run occurs in the extent to which the two parts of the proceeding are merged and the associated use of the SER. In the case of the rarely used procedures for applications to discharge or vary a care order and those related to opposed S2 resolutions there is real uncertainty and variability in practice. Clarification of procedures in these areas would probably be helpful.

In all the proceedings in the juvenile court there is a second main area of variability, namely in the part played by the parents. In quite a number of courts the role of the parents extends considerably beyond 'rebutting allegations' as specified in the Magistrates Court Rules. In some they are accorded the status of full parties to the proceedings: either the parent or a solicitor on his behalf calls witnesses, cross-examines witnesses and addresses the court on the full range of matters raised. In other courts the parents are not prevented from taking part. In practice this usually means that they are called as witnesses or are asked if they have anything to say. In a few courts their role is strictly limited. There is a widespread belief among solicitors, social workers and others associated with the court that the restricted role of the parents is unjust and does not promote perceived justice. Many believe that they should be made parties to the proceedings and entitled to legal aid. Some courts are obviously prepared to use their discretion and give parents a much greater opportunity to take part.

Both solicitors and social workers expressed dissatisfaction with the way the court works. About half the social workers interviewed felt that the court did usually operate in the best interests of the child, although half of this group mentioned limitations such as the setting, the procedures and the restricted disposal options. Thirty-five percent said that they thought the court did not act in the child's interests. Social workers were particularly concerned about the 'criminal' associations which pervade care proceedings and the way parents and children perceive the hearing and the decision. A significant number also referred to the variability in court's practice and decisions as a regrettable feature of the system. A rather larger proportion of the sample of solicitors were critical of the juvenile court (60%). They commented that the lay magistracy is not really equipped to deal with the complex legal and psychological issues raised in child care cases and that the bench tends to be overimpressed with the professional expertise of the local authority. They felt that in practice the court acts as a rubber stamp for decisions taken by the local authority. In support of this view they commented on how infrequently the court disagrees with the social worker's recommendation.

The main reservation which social workers and solicitors raise about the juvenile court are considered in greater detail below:

1. The setting and style of court hearings

Many social workers are concerned that care proceedings are imbued with connotations of punishment. The formality of the physical setting and its associations with criminal prosecutions were adversely commented on by 53% of social workers; 64% wanted to see changes in the formality of the procedures and style and 47% criticised the confusion of criminal and care cases in the courthouse. Many social workers are themselves uncomfortable with the setting and style of the court and believe that both parents and children find the court overpowering and alienating. They also expressed concern over the restricted part parents could play. Even when the parents are encouraged to take part unfamiliarity with the place, the strangeness of the procedures and the emphasis on verbal and intellectual skills severely limits their effective contribution. Under these circumstances it was felt that parents often did not understand what had happened, felt that they had been excluded and had not had a fair hearing. Both parents and children often saw a care order as a form of punishment for some poorly understood shortcoming. Some social workers went so far as to say that the court proceedings could make it extremely difficult to work with a family subsequently because of the hostility and distrust created. This possibility had to be taken into account when deciding whether or not to take proceedings.

Solicitors, being more familiar with the court setting, are relatively unaware of the effects of the physical environment on newcomers. Some, however, are in favour of a reduction in the formality of the procedures (9) and greater flexibility about who can take part (60% wanted to see the parents entitled to play a greater part). A number supported the idea that all family matters should be dealt with by the same court (8) and clearly separated from criminal cases (4).

The desirability of informality of the setting and procedures in the juvenile court is perhaps less straightforward than it appears. When business has to be conducted between a relatively large group of people there is normally a strong element of structure. The fact that the structure is not explicit is sometimes mistaken for informality. The perceived formality of a setting is often more a matter of experience and associations than inherent in its structural characteristics. Thus a social worker expressing the wish that court hearings be conducted in the manner of a round table discussion in an office or committee room may be simply reflecting the fact that this would be an environment familiar to him and where, perhaps without knowing it, he knows the structure and the rules. Such a structure may be no more familiar or 'including' to a parent involved in care proceedings than a magistrates court.

Formal settings and procedures have advantages which should not be ignored. First, formality of a conventional kind conveys authority. An appropriate setting for care proceedings should make it clear that the matters under discussion are extremely serious and the decisions of the court have the force of law. To give any other impression would be misleading. Second, formal procedures have normally evolved in a way which attempts to counter-act certain fallibilities in human information processing and decision-making. For example, adversarial procedures can be an effective way of counteracting

the tendency to select and perceive information in the light of a compelling point of view. In a less formal setting there may be no-one who will argue the alternative view, perceive the weaknesses in a case or draw attention to discrepant facts. This may be so because no-one perceives the need to do so or because there are pressures within the group to minimize conflict and argument. When decision-making is conducted informally and without explicit procedures, as for example in case conferences, there is always the risk that information will be omitted, conflict concealed and there will be disputes afterwards about what was agreed.

The physical circumstances in which care proceedings are heard, the waiting areas and the scheduling of cases in relation to criminal cases are matters which if given greater attention could significantly improve the experience of those attending court and their perception of the nature of the proceedings. This particularly applies to parents and children, but also applies to social workers and other witnesses. Any move to a less formal procedure should, however, be considered very carefully. From observing juvenile court hearings in contrasting physical settings it is our impression that the hearings conducted in a comfortable, modern room of moderate size are much more acceptable than those conducted in formal courtrooms using exactly the same procedure. The setting appears to influence both the style adopted by court personnel and the perception of participants such as social workers and parents.

2. The independence of court decisions

In total, 53 cases in the sample involved a full hearing in the juvenile court. In only 4 of these cases did the decision of the court not accord with the case or the recommendations put to the court by the social services department:
- 1 case was found not proved;
- in 2 cases a supervision order was made where a care order had been recommended;
- in 1 case an application for discharge of a care order was dismissed when the social worker had recommended replacing a care order with a supervision order.

It was thus unusual for the court to disagree with the assessment of the case by the social services department. It is impossible to assess whether a 'failure rate' of about 10% is too high or too low. From the social services point of view it can be argued that the percentage should be low since cases are discussed extensively by a range of people before they are taken to court. In addition, cases will not be taken to court if there are serious doubts about whether there is adequate evidence. (Several cases in the sample were not pursued for this reason.) It follows that only 'strong' cases are ever taken to court.

Many of the private solicitors interviewed expressed reservations about the independence of the court. Some believed that when cases are brought to court by the local authority they carry with them a presumption of proof. A few were particularly concerned that once a place of safety order had been made the burden of proof fell firmly on the respondent. Solicitors argue that magistrates are naturally aware of the extensive decision-making process within the local authority and the professional expertise which the social

services calls on in making decisions. Inevitably they must assume, it is argued, that good grounds must exist for the local authority to bring a case before them. Some solicitors feel that lay magistrates are unwilling to criticise the professional judgement of social workers or to challenge them when they carry so much responsibility for the welfare of children. Without the discipline provided by a thorough training in either the law or child development they are thought to be vulnerable to personal or local influences in their assessments of the evidence and the opinions of social workers.

Not unnaturally most social workers do not see the matter in this way. A few (12) said that they thought the court was too influenced by the social worker's recommendation. Others felt that magistrates could be too influenced by their personal and social attitudes and be too susceptible to local pressures. However in general social workers significantly overestimate the probability of 'losing' a case. The few instances where the court overrules their recommendation loom large in their thinking and tend to overshadow the vast majority where the decision is in their favour.

It is, of course, not only magistrates who may be impressed by the local authority's expertise and professional assessment. Solicitors too may hold their judgements in high regard. Solicitors trying to represent children may well feel that the social workers probably know what is best for children. Solicitors have no training or expertise in the field themselves and few have access to anyone who does have these skills. In about one third of the care proceedings cases in the sample the solicitor for the child supported the recommendations put forward by the social worker. Sometimes the solicitor had obviously made up his mind before the case came to court and made his position known to the court at the beginning of the hearing. Where a solicitor does this and consequently fails to put the local authority's case to the test it could be argued that he is helping to deprive the court of its independence.

From our observations of juvenile court hearings we believed that in some cases there was reason to doubt that the court was acting as an independent decision-making body. Where the time spent hearing a case was very short it seemed reasonable to suppose that the decision was little more than a formality; 7 of the 33 observed cases took ½ hour or less to hear including 2 which took less than 10 minutes. Secondly, when the facts and disposition stages of the case were not separated the onus of proof seemed to lie with the parents rather than the local authority; that is, there tended to be a presumption of proof of the local authority's case. Rather than the responsibility falling on the local authority in the first instance to prove its case on the facts, the early introduction of the social worker's opinions and judgements placed the parents or child in the position of having to prove that the professional's judgement was wrong. Unless they have access to pro-fessional advisors themselves there is very little chance of them being successful in such a challenge. The advantage thus lies with the professionals. Lack of separation of the two phases was observed in one third of the cases. On these two grounds we felt that there was reason to be concerned about the independence of the court's decision in half the cases we observed.

The role which solicitors adopt in a hearing can make a considerable impact on the court. In many cases it depends on whether the solicitor for the child

takes an active part in testing the evidence put forward by the local authority and whether he calls his own witnesses as to how thoroughly the case is examined. Since the juvenile court is not inquisitorial in style it is the advocates who must bring out the information which the court needs to make a decision. Occasionally magistrates themselves seek information, but this is comparatively rare. (The role played by solicitors is examined further in a latter section.)

In this discussion the functioning of the juvenile court has been considered in relation to the criteria of the court as an independent decision-making body. We have argued that the independence of the court is in jeopardy if the procedures are not followed, particularly if the separation of the two stages are not maintained; if the solicitors pre-empt the decision of the court by supporting the local authority recommendation from the start; or if the case is not thoroughly presented or tested. In those cases where we observed the procedures being followed and the advocates taking an active part in testing the case, it appeared that, at least at the level of the information presented and in terms of a 'fair hearing', the court did act as an independent decision-making body.

3. Limited disposal options

A number of solicitors and social workers felt that the juvenile court was less effective than it should be because of the limited options available for dealing with a case. The decision of the court is in practice limited to whether or not to make a care order. Supervision orders are not often made in care proceedings except in 'education cases'. In those cases where supervision orders were made, there was a strong suspicion that they were used where a case had not really been proved rather than as an appropriate disposal of a proved case. The inability of the court to specify any of the aspects of the management of a child on a care order is seen by some solicitors and magistrates as a serious limitation on the court's ability to make an appropriate response to the particular circumstances of a case. Some also regretted the fact that the court cannot initiate a review of a case at a later date.

The lack of disposal options affects the proceedings in a number of ways. First, it contributes to the tendency to blur the two stages of the proceedings because the decisions in the two stages are not distinct; finding the case proved is tantamount to deciding to make a care order. Second, solicitors feel that their role in representing the interests of their clients, whether parents or children, is significantly impaired because they cannot try to ensure that specific provisions are made, e.g. access of parents, specific placement of the child or provision for rehabilitation. They also argue that it is unreasonable to try to make an assessment of the best interests of the child if they cannot consider the care that will be provided by the local authority. Because no formal arrangements can be made in relation to those aspects of the child's future care which are of greatest importance to the child or the parents, attempts may be made to deal with these matters informally. In some cases we observed, either the parents' or the child's solicitor withdrew their opposition to a care order being made on the informal understanding that certain

arrangements would be made about, for example, returning the child home. It is doubtful whether agreements which are as important as this should be left to informal processes; misunderstandings can so easily occur; the temptation is created to make implied promises which are unlikely to materialise; there is no redress if the informal agreements are not kept. In some cases, the wish to deal with these questions was evident in that questions were asked of the social worker (or social services representative) by both the magistrates and solicitors about the placement of the child. Occasionally magistrates specified certain management provision in making an order.

One further effect of the lack of disposal options in care proceedings is on the decision-making process prior to the hearing. Because the arrangements for the care of the child are not questioned in court, there is no incentive for the social services to make plans for the future care of the child at an early stage. Except in cases where the application for a care order is contingent on a suitable placement being available, placement planning is often deferred until after the order has been obtained.

As was seen in the decisions made in the wardship cases in the sample, the ability of the high court to make more complex provisions seems to result in orders being made which are suited to the needs of the case. As they are often based on pre-hearing negotiations, they are also acceptable to all parties. If the specific provisions made do not work in practice, they can be reviewed by the court at a later date. This flexibility is widely agreed to be the main advantage of wardship proceedings.

We would argue that an increased range of orders which could be made by the juvenile court or provisions which could be specified would have important effects on many aspects of the system. The court might be given the powers to specify for example, access of parents, the child's return home for holidays or weekends, review by the court after a set period, etc. A greater range of options would place greater emphasis on the professional placement management aspects in the social enquiry report and help to separate this aspect of the report from the report as a proof of evidence. It would provide an incentive to the social services to make plans for the placement and care of the child as part of the decision-making stage in a case. It would give greater distinction to the two stages of care proceedings and would give greater scope to the role of the representative of the child.

Solicitors

The role of the representative of the child in care proceedings is poorly defined and a source of considerable doubt and confusion both to solicitors and social workers. It seemed to us that few solicitors had thought their way through the complexities of their role to a viable professional stance. This was evident both in the responses obtained in interviews and from observing solicitors in court. Perhaps a quarter of those interviewed could not describe the role even in task terms. About one third of the solicitors observed in court appeared to have little to contribute to the proceedings. Some solicitors seemed to take on too little in their role, remaining very passive and making only minimal efforts in

preparing and developing the case. Others took on too much, becoming too dependent on the social services department and judging the case in advance. Some solicitors become very emotionally involved in these cases, with their personal feelings completely overwhelming their professional detachment. We met several solicitors who were not prepared to continue doing child care cases because they found them too distressing. The situation is clearly one where the professional role definition is not providing a containing structure which allows a degree of involvement with the issues without complete personal immersion. Of course some solicitors have developed a satisfactory definition of the role for themselves. They are, however, probably not in a majority. The profession has given little or no help in providing training, forums for debate or published literature. (One exception is the course on Advocacy in the Juvenile Court organised by the Legal Action Group).

The central role problem for the solicitor is the nature and extent of his decision-making function. How far should a solicitor representing a child be involved in deciding what is best for the child? A professional derives his authority for his decisions from the body of knowledge of the profession and his independence from administrative pressure. (See discussions on professions for example, Greenwood (1957), Wilensky (1964)). For a solicitor the profession's body of knowledge does not include the care and development of children. He can of course seek advice from professionals who do have that expertise but in order to protect his independence it is doubtful whether that advice should be sought from the social worker who is the representative of the local authority bringing the action. The social worker is an important source of information but should probably not be depended on as a professional adviser.

Whether or not the solicitor has the advice which would allow him to make an assessment of the merits of the care order, it can be argued that he does have a responsibility to his client to see that the applicant's case is proved. Since his client, the child, cannot instruct him to forego the need to prove the case (as an adult in a criminal case can decide to plead guilty) he always has the responsibility to test the local authority's case. In order to ensure that the case is tested, he should never say that he will support the making of a care order before the case is proved. In fact, he may need to approach the matter from the stance of 'opposing the case' in order to see that the relevant information is brought out in court. It is the court who has the public sanction to make the decisions in the case and this is where the responsibility should ultimately lie.

The role of the solicitor representing the child becomes particularly difficult when the parents are not represented, and more so if he comes to represent the child as the result of an approach from the parents. Although he may have no professional responsibility to the parents, he may feel responsible towards them since the law has deprived them of the right to be legally represented in care proceedings. The views of the parents can be investigated by the solicitor and introduced into court as part of the information relevant to the case. It does, however, demand considerable intellectual detachment for the presentation of the views of the parents to be kept distinct from representing their point of view. Social workers observing solicitors do not believe that the separation can in fact be maintained. Separate representation for parents is

probably the only way the solicitor for the child can be relieved of the pressure to represent the parents' point of view.

The arguments that the parents should be made party to care proceedings, be entitled to be represented and to receive legal aid, are strong and widely supported by both solicitors and social workers. Many are critical that the provisions in the Children's Act 1975 have not been implemented to date. It is normally the parents and not the child who are opposed to the application for a care order and have an alternative view to be put to the court. Making an order will affect their legal rights over their children. In the interests of perceived justice, the protection of parents' legal rights and ensuring that all relevant matters are put to the court there seems to be good reasons to support parents being represented. There may of course be reluctance to extend the legal aid provisions at the present time because of expense. In the meantime, it could be made clear that the parents should be encouraged to take as full a part as possible in the proceedings and that they should be given advice and help on the nature of the proceedings and the way they can contribute.

Social workers and the decision to take proceedings

Because of the high 'success rate' of applications to the juvenile court, the decision to take proceedings is of crucial importance. Partly as a result of the publicity given to the Maria Colwell case and later cases in which a child died, there is a high level of concern for the safety of children both in general and in the responsible agencies. Decisions to take action in relation to a child are often made in the face of real or perceived crises. A child being removed from home on a place of safety order is a common feature of cases and the child being thought to be at risk is frequently an element in the decision. Cases are more often brought under S.1.2.a) proper development grounds than any of the other grounds for care proceedings. There is now some concern expressed, for example by social services management, that the high level of anxiety about the risk of violence to children has led to an over-reaction. There is thought to be a 'safety first' policy particularly among agencies who are not responsible for providing for the subsequent care of the child.

The widespread practice of calling multi-agency case conferences in all cases where a child is thought to be at risk has in some ways contributed to this trend. Despite advice to keep the membership of these conferences down, the pressure to include anyone with any interest in the case leads to conferences being held which are too large. This is particularly true for non-accidental injury conferences. In large conferences the dynamics of the group are of considerable importance. For example, it is difficult for the members of so large a group not to regard the conference as the decision-making body. There are strong pressures to operate in a consensus mode and to conceal conflict. The over-representation of a particular interest group (either by the numbers, the seniority or the forcefulness of participants) can determine the whole pattern of discussion.

This study did not consider the practice of case conferences in detail and we are not in a position to evaluate their effectiveness in the decision-making

process. However, there were cases looked at in the study in which the use of the case conference did not seem entirely satisfactory. In several cases there were repeated conferences: having another conference seemed to be used as the substitute, and a very expensive one, for making a decision. In one instance the seriousness implied by calling a conference of fifteen people appeared to prevent the group agreeing that there were really no grounds on which to take any action. In one or two cases there were indications that the conference had come to an exaggerated view of the seriousness of the case which could not later be substantiated in court. In two cases there were major conflicts in view which were not dealt with in the conference and led to serious breaches in the relationships between the agencies who disagreed. From this limited material it seems to us that the case conference is not always the best way of handling inter-agency communication and decisions in relation to child care cases and that work should be done to develop a wider range of alternative procedures.

In most of the care proceedings hearings which we observed no mention was made of whether a case conference had been held. However, in several cases heard in the London court the magistrate asked whether a case conference had been held and what had been its recommendation. Information from lawyers working in London suggest that this practice is not uncommon in other London courts. Since case conferences are primarily information-sharing mechanisms and are not governed by any procedure which checks the reliability of the information put forward, it does not seem desirable for the court to know the outcome of a conference or even that one has been held. For a lay magistrate to know that fifteen or so professionals from a wide range of disciplines have discussed the matter and come to a conclusion is unlikely to be an encouragement to independent decision-making by the court.

The fact that a case will have to be heard by a court if it is proceeded with has observable effects on the decision-making of the local authority. First, there are cases where no further action is taken because it is believed that the evidence would not be acceptable to the court. This usually follows advice given by the local authority solicitor but may be decided by the social worker alone. Thus, even without hearing the case, the court acts as a form of control on the decision-making process. A similar phenomenon occurs with the high court: the court hearing provides an incentive for the parties to reach an agreement which they would not have otherwise have been prepared to make. Secondly, the orientation of the decision-making towards a court hearing sometimes concentrates attention on the mechanics of obtaining an order and away from a consideration of the purpose of a care order and planning for the care of the child. This was clearly demonstrated in one case conference in which the social workers, doctors, and other professionals spent most of the time discussing the orders to obtain on each of the children concerned and the likely response of the court, while the local authority lawyer argued that if they decided on what they wanted to achieve with the family he would make sure the appropriate legal orders were obtained. As has been observed above, explicit planning of future care was not a feature of many of the cases studied. We have argued that giving the court a greater range of disposal options would contribute to an improvement in professional practice in this regard.

If the period from the decision to intervene up to and including the court

hearing is seen as a series of stages in a decision-making process with different tasks and roles associated with each stage, it becomes apparent that the role demands on social workers are complex. This is most evident where the local authority is making the application. It is hard to think of another type of legal procedure where the same person is the client, that is the person who decides that the action be taken and instructs the solicitor, the main and sometimes only witness and the principal professional adviser to the court. In addition, this same person may take on aspects of the role normally played by the solicitor in case preparation and may also have responsibilities in relation to resource provision once an order is obtained. There are, of course, substantial areas of overlap between these roles. The communalities between the roles encourage their identification with the same person in each case, namely the social worker. However, they do have elements which are distinct. The roles have somewhat different objectives and the role holders are therefore subject to different pressures. For example, as a representative of the social services the social worker is under pressure to protect a child from harm; as a provider or resources he is under pressure not to oversubscribe scarce resources or curtail the decisions regarding those resources; as an adviser to the court he has a professional responsibility to make and present an independent assessment of a child's situation; as an applicant to the court with the backing of a case conference he has the objective of winning his case. When all the roles are performed by the same person it is not surprising if that person is seen by others as having too much power, or of confusing the interests of one role with those of another. In particular, his credibility as an independent, professional adviser to the court is seriously at risk.

In discussing child care cases and the courts with social workers we found that, in general, they were relatively unaware of the role complexities implicit in these kinds of cases. However, there were indications that they do experience role stress and role conflict. First, many expressed uncertainty and anxiety about taking cases to court either because of the nature of the court hearings themselves or because of doubts about whether the child's interests would be best served in this way. Second, the criticisms of the system or suggestions for change made by social workers tended to be those which would reduce the complexities or conflicts inherent in their own roles, for example, the wish that juvenile court hearings should be conducted as round table discussions. Third, tension or disagreements in relationships with other professionals or agencies, including both the local authority and private solicitors, seemed to arise out of or as a projection of conflicts in the social worker's role.

It is perhaps not surprising that social workers do not have well developed role concepts in relation to child care cases. They appear to be given little formal training in this area and cases involving court hearings are comparatively rare in the experience of many. To some extent the need for supports for social workers has been recognised and a range of informal systems have been developed. (These were reviewed in detail in Chapter IV). The development has however been patchy, with some areas having made quite sophisticated provisions and others little or none. In considering how these systems should be developed in future, we would make the following suggestions:

1. Training

More training in the law is seen by many social workers as an appropriate remedy for their uncertainties in this area. While social workers do need to know the broad provisions of the Acts, it is probably undesirable for them to become too immersed in the detail. The local authority's legal department is there to provide detailed knowledge. They do, however, need training courses and materials in the principles and purposes of the legal machinery and procedures and, following that, in the roles which the various participants need to perform.

Recently there has been a commendable increase in the range of relatively straightforward publications on child law intended for social workers (e.g. Feldman (1978); Hoggett (1977); Raisbeck (1977)). However, in general these books are too concerned with legal detail to be of much help to social workers not dealing adequately with the use of the law and their relationship to it.

Short courses run in conjunction with courts are valuable and should be more widely available. The development of courses and course material on writing social enquiry reports would also be highly desirable. Informal meetings, courses or discussions which draw attention to the issues raised in child care proceedings can also make a significant contribution to raising awareness and concentrating attention on this aspect of social work and the roles of social workers.

2. Support Personnel

The courts officer, at least in those areas where the role is well developed, can make a significant contribution to maintaining and co-ordinating the relationship between social services departments and the courts, and sometimes with the legal department, solicitors and the police. Those areas with a less elaborate system may wish to look at the experience and practice of other departments. However, there is always a danger that concentrating expertise in one or two specialists will detract from the grassroots knowledge of field staff. At least one area did not have a courts officer for this reason. Also, the balance of responsibilities for supervision between the courts officer and team leaders has not always been established satisfactorily.

3. Social Enquiry Reports

From an analysis of the content and use of the social enquiry report we concluded that there is a real need for a major development exercise to be carried out in this area. The social enquiry report exemplifies many of the confusions which are characteristic of the social worker's roles. The confusions in the roles are played out in the social enquiry report, and the social enquiry report further confuses and merges the roles, thus creating a feedback system. If the roles were clarified and ways found of separating and containing some of the elements, then the problems with the social enquiry report would tend to disappear. Alternatively, we would suggest that working on the social enquiry report could provide a point of focus for examining the role issues within a bounded and externalised development task.

4. Relationships with Private Solicitors

There are considerable differences between individuals and between areas in the way social workers relate to private solicitors. There is also uncertainty as to how the relationship should be conducted. What information the social worker should provide to the solicitor and how he subsequently uses that information are central unresolved questions in the relationship. Neither the uncertainty nor the differences in practice are really satisfactory for either side. However, significant improvement is probably contingent on a clarification of the roles both of solicitors and social workers. While social workers are unclear about their own roles in relation to court proceedings, they are unlikely to develop an understanding of the role played by the solicitor. Without such an understanding, their response to requests for information will continue to be determined more by person-based than role-based relationships. At present a social worker's response to a solicitor is unpredictable: at one extreme he may withhold information without which the solicitor cannot perform any function; at the other he may do his best to convert the solicitor to the social worker's view of the case. Since the solicitor for the child does not usually have any other source of professional advice, he depends on the social worker for basic information and professional expertise. Unless the solicitor has a well developed concept of his role as the representative of the child, he may drift into over-dependence on the social worker.

Despite the need for overall role clarification, two particular issues should be given immediate attention. First, what is the proper role of the social worker (or social services department representative) in obtaining representation for a child? In cases where the parent has made no arrangements for the child to be represented and the child is in the care of the local authority (for example on a place of safety or interim care order), perhaps it should be the social worker's responsibility to see that the child is represented. However, it is probably not desirable for the social services to have any part in approaching or naming a particular solicitor. For solicitors to become in any way dependent on the social services for work must endanger their real or perceived independence. Ideally, the responsibility for seeing that the child is represented should be handled entirely and automatically by the court. Second, social workers might be helped if area officers or social services departments developed a policy on what kind of information could be communicated to the solicitor for the child and the solicitor for the parent. In particular, thought should be given to the availability of the social enquiry report. While some social workers argue that the social enquiry report is a report to the court and only the court can decide to whom it shall be given, solicitors representing the child quite reasonably point out that they cannot make an assessment of the case without adequate time to consider the social enquiry report. Developing the content and structure of the social enquiry report, as discussed above, could go some way to resolving this problem. If it were decided that the information given to a solicitor should be limited, this could result in some solicitors obtaining less information than they do at present through informal means. However, formalising the arrangements would make it clear to solicitors what they could expect and perhaps encourage

them to make their own investigations and if necessary seek independent advice.

5. Relationships with the local authority solicitor

In considering the relationship between social workers and the local authority legal department, the study was limited by there being only one, or ocassionally two solicitors handling child care cases in each of the five authorities. The way the work was organised and the role defined was different in each authority. It is, therefore, difficult to draw conclusions on the basis of this limited sample. However, there were indications that the relationship sometimes gives rise to tensions and misunderstandings. Despite signs of strain, there appeared to have been little explicit consideration of the inter-departmental relationship except in one authority. In this one instance the relationship had been given attention jointly by the legal department and the social services department as a result of dissatisfaction with past arrangements. With a growing case load, increasingly complex law and greater public concern about cases involving children being taken into care, co-ordination and mutual understanding between departments has become more important. The relationship has come under greater pressure without work having been done to examine and strengthen it. In the authority where the relationship had been considered by both departments, the current situation seemed much more satisfactory, certainly to the social services department.

Social workers' expectations of the extent of the service the department can and should provide and the role the solicitor should play have remained implicit rather than explicit. Whether these expectations are consonant with the solicitors' views of their role has generally not been tested. Thus the role perceptions are sometimes not shared and dissatisfactions arise when unspoken or inconsistent expectations are not met. The procedures for communicating information and allocating tasks and responsibilities are generally unspecified. Currently the burden of conducting and developing the relationship lies with the solicitor. However, these activities are not emphasised by legal department management and relevant skills do not seem to be used as criteria for selecting solicitors to work on child care cases.

We would suggest that joint work by the legal department and the social services department on developing even elementary procedures and mechanisms for conducting the relationship between them would be of great value, when this has not already occurred. The procedures might be concerned with, for example, how and when the legal department should be involved in case decisions, responsiblities for various aspects of case preparation, mechanisms for handling complaints about how cases were presented. Working on these issues would provide an opportunity to consider mutual expectations and perceptions. In addition, the availability of such procedures would help social workers, particularly those who are inexperienced in child care cases, to direct their attention to legal aspects of a case and tasks which would need to be carried out. For example, if a form were used to notify the legal department about a case which asked for information not only about the

reasons for taking action but also who could give evidence on that point, the form itself would draw attention to the need for first-hand evidence in making a case. If such a form also asked for the name and address of the solicitor representing the child, this would constitute a reminder that someone would need to check and possibly arrange such representation.

The other persistent problem in the inter-departmental relationship which emerged even in the small number of cases examined, was the discontinuity in the personnel handling child care cases in legal departments. The present organization of legal departments, the career progression of local authority lawyers and the expectations of mobility among solicitors seem to make it unlikely that the wish of social workers for continuity can be met without major structural change. While it would be desirable for welfare law generally to achieve higher status within the legal profession and thus attract and retain staff, such changes in legal attitudes will only happen slowly. Without major change, the situation would certainly be improved if the change-over between one solicitor and another could be handled more smoothly. For example, the transition period should probably be at least six months where possible and greater efforts should be made to provide opportunities for area offices, and particularly key people such as courts officers and team leaders, to get to know a solicitor starting to take up child care cases.

Children who are subjects of proceedings

As was mentioned above, this study was not designed to evaluate the decisions made to take proceedings or the decisions of the court in terms of the care provided for children. However, during the discussion of the way the system works in practice there were some features relating to children which should be drawn out in conclusion.

In a large number of the cases studied the child was removed from home at the outset and placed in a temporary setting. Such a move involves a major upheaval for a child, particularly a very young child, disrupting his relationships with adults probably more than once. There would seem to be a strong case for limiting the amount of disruption as much as possible and resolving uncertainty with the minimum delay. As was shown in the analysis of the cases, it is not uncommon for cases to take two months to come to court and some take considerably longer. During that time the child may be placed in one or sometimes more temporary arrangements, and even infants may be placed in residential homes, although short-term fostering is more common for young children. In some cases delays arise because of the nature of the case itself, for example, the need for assessment of the child or instability in the family situation. However, in other cases the delay is the result of administrative or organisational factors. The longest delays occur in wardship cases, sometimes as a result of the length of time taken to obtain reports, or in cases where criminal charges are brought against the parents in relation to the child. Lack of availability of court dates was a major contributor to delays in some cases and reflects the lack of priority given to care cases. The failure to organise representation or to ensure the availability of witnesses or parents contributed

to delays of two to three months in some cases. In these instances, inefficiencies caused by lack of more developed role definitions and clear allocation of tasks between role holders appear to have operated to adversely affect the child who was the subject of the proceedings.

We have argued that the system as it is currently organized and operated gives little encouragement to social workers and social services departments to place greater emphasis on developing plans for the child's future or to consider carefully what will be achieved by obtaining a care order. These matters may, of course, be considered and in some cases are of great importance. However, the system itself is geared towards placing an emphasis on the justification for intervention rather than what intervention would achieve, in the decision to take proceedings. Once such a decision is made, the system encourages the applicant to concentrate on the mechanics and tactics of obtaining an order rather than on planning for and providing care for the child. Only by giving the court who is responsible for these decisions greater options and powers in making and reviewing orders will the central issue of the hearing become predominant, namely the best interests and future care of the child.

References

Anderson, R. (1977) *Representation in the Juvenile Court*. Routledge and Kegan Paul. London.

Baldwin, J. and McConville, M (1977) *Negotiated Justice*. Martin Robertson. London.

Central Council for Education and Training in Social Work. (1974) *Social Work: The Social Worker and the Courts*. Paper 7.

DHSS (1974) *Report of the Committee of Inquiry Into the Care and Supervision Provided in Relation to Maria Colwell*. HMSO London.

Du Cann, R. (1980) *The Art of the Advocate*. Penguin, London.

Eekelaar, J. M. (1977) Children in Care and the Children's Act. 1975. *Mod. Law Rev.*. 40, 2, 121 – 140.

Feldman, L. (1976) Preparing a Case: Children in Care—5. *LAG Bull*. November, 249.

Feldman, Linda (1978) *Care Proceedings*. Oyez. London

Great Britain (1960) *Report of the Committee on Children and Young Persons* under the Chairmanship of Viscount Ingleby. HMSO London.

Greenwood, E. (1957) Attributes of a Profession. *Soc. Work*. 2, 45 – 55.

Halle, H. C. and Stevenson, O. (1980) *Child Abuse*: aspects of interprofessional co-operation. Allen and Unwin. London.

Hayes, M. (1978) Separate representation of children in care proceedings. *Fam. Law*. 8, 3, 91 – 96.

Hilgendorf, E. L. (1978) Social Work as a Profession. *T.I.H.R. Report*, No. 2T178

Hoggett, Brenda (1977) *Parents and Children*. Sweet and Maxwell. London.

Lowe, N. V. and White R. A. H. (1979) *Wards of Court*. Butterworths, London.

McClean, J. D. (1978) *Karen Spencer*. Derbyshire County Court.

Morris, A. and Giller, H. (1977) The Juvenile Court: the Client's Perspective. *Crim. Law. Rev.*.

Morris, A., Giller, H., Szwed, E. and Geach, H. (1980) *Justice for Children*. Macmillans. London.

Moss, G. and Sutton, A. (1981) Educational Psychologists and the juvenile court. In Lloyd-Bostock, S. *Law and Psychology*. Socio-legal Studies, Oxford.

Priestly, P., Fears, D. and Fuller, R. (1977) *Justice for Juveniles*. Routledge and Kegan Paul. London.

Raisbeck, B. L. *Law and the Social Worker*. MacMillan Press. London.

Somerset Area Review Committee (1977) *Wayne Brewer: Report of the Review Panel*.

Taylor, L., Lacey, R. and Bracken, D. (1979) *In Whose Best Interests*? Cobden Trust and MIND. London.

Wilensky, Harold L. (1964) 'The Professionalisation of Everyone?' *American Journal of Sociology*. 70, 137 – 158.

Printed in England for Her Majesty's Stationery Office by Hobbs the Printers of Southampton
(1355) Dd717213 C20 10/81 G381